YOUR
ADVERSARY
D THE EVIL

Your Adversary the Devil

J. Dwight Pentecost

kregel
PUBLICATIONS

Grand Rapids, MI 49501

Your Adversary, the Devil

Copyright © 1969 by J. Dwight Pentecost

Published in 1997 by Kregel Publications, a division of
Kregel, Inc., P.O. Box 2607, Grand Rapids, MI 49501.
Kregel Publications provides trusted, biblical publications for
Christian growth and service. Your comments and sugges-
tions are valued.

Cover photo: Copyright © 1997 PhotoDisc, vol. 1
Cover design: Alan G. Hartman

Library of Congress Cataloging-in-Publication Data
Pentecost, J. Dwight.
    Your adversary, the Devil / J. Dwight Pentecost.
        p.   cm.
    Originally published: Grand Rapids, Mich.: Zondervan
Publishing House, 1969.
    1. Devil—Biblical teaching. 2. Devil—History of
doctrines. 3. Good and evil—Biblical teaching. I. Title.
BT981.P46   1997   235'.4—dc21   96-46395
                                                                CIP
ISBN 0-8254-3455-6

Printed in the United States of America

1 2 3 / 03 02 01 00 99 98 97

TO MY WIFE
*who stands alongside
in the battle*

Contents

Introduction

No military commander could expect to be victorious in battle unless he understood his enemy. Should he prepare for an attack by land and ignore the possibility that the enemy might approach by air or by sea, he would open the way to defeat. Or should he prepare for a land and sea attack and ignore the possibility of an attack through the air, he would certainly jeopardize the campaign.

No individual can be victorious against the adversary of our souls unless he understands that adversary; unless he understands his philosophy, his methods of operation, his methods of temptation. We hear very little today about Satan, and consequently many who recognize Satan's existence and acknowledge that he is the enemy of their souls are ill-prepared to meet him. We are ignorant of the nature of this one who comes knocking at our heart's door. We do not know what Scripture teaches about his person, his methods, his plans, his program, his devices. Consequently we fall in defeat.

How foolish it would be for a doctor who has discovered lung cancer in a patient to prescribe a corn plaster for application to his little toe. The treatment must fit the disease. If we are going to be victorious in the warfare into which we were thrust the moment we accepted Jesus Christ as Saviour, we need to understand that large body of Scripture that reveals to us the person and the work of the one with whom we are at war. It is our desire to examine the Scriptures to learn from their extensive revelation the nature of our adversary, the Devil, his devices, deceits, doctrines, designs — so that we may detect his movements in our daily experience. Victory may be ours. But victory depends on knowledge. We trust that these words may be used by the Victor to bring us to victory.

Grateful acknowledgment is made and deep thanks offered to Miss Nancy Miller and Mrs. Reba Allen for their invaluable help, given as unto the Lord, in the work preparing this manuscript for publication. Without their labors this volume would not have been published. May the Lord grant them great joy as He is pleased to use this in which they had a significant part to spread the knowledge of His victory.

J. DWIGHT PENTECOST

Dallas, Texas

1

The Fall of Satan

Ezekiel 28:11 - 27

Where did Satan come from? Did God create the Devil? Is God responsible for evil? Such questions plague the individual who wrestles with the existence of our adversary in the light of the Bible's revelation of the holiness of God. Philosophy can never give a satisfactory answer to these questions. The only satisfying answer is God's answer found in His Word.

In Ezekiel 25 - 32 the prophet is pronouncing judgment on many of Israel's enemies. He describes God's divine judgment on nations that have persecuted Israel. In Chapter 28 verses 1 to 10 he has delivered a message of judgment against the land of Tyre. Tyre, a part of the biblical Syria to the north, occupied by the Phoenicians, one of Israel's chief enemies. But in verses 11 to 17 he moves beyond the physical "prince of Tyre," the king of that nation, and addresses a word concerning judgment on the one who controlled the "prince of Tyre." This one is called the king of Tyre. We should observe that Satan works through men. He works through governmental leaders on many occasions. Because Satan desired to exterminate Israel so that God's Messiah could not come to bless the earth through that nation, he stirred up Gentile nations against Israel. Those Gentiles in persecuting and seeking to exterminate Israel were working out the philosophy and program of Satan without recognizing or realizing it. So as the prophet pronounces judgment upon this enemy of Israel in verses 1 - 10, he moves on to speak a word of judgment upon the one who controlled these gentile princes.

11

The one whom we call Satan was originally known by the name of Lucifer, which means, "the light bearer," or "the brilliant one," "the shining one." In Ezekiel 28:11-13 we discover why that name was so appropriate. The prophet begins his judgment by saying, "take up a lamentation upon the king of Tyre [that is upon Satan himself] and say unto him, Thus saith the Lord God; Thou sealest up the sum, full of wisdom, and perfect in beauty." Verse 12 describes for us something of the perfection of Lucifer before his fall.

Lucifer was a created being. That is pointed out to us in the 15th verse. "Thou wast perfect in thy ways from the day that thou wast created, till iniquity was found in thee." God alone is eternal. God alone possesses eternal, or uncreated life. All else that lives, lives because God created it. All created things have a different kind of life than God has, a created kind of life. And God in His work of creation began by creating an innumerable host of angelic beings one of which was Lucifer. As a creature he was obliged to worship and serve and obey the Creator. Satan was not created the arch fiend that he has become by his rebellion. The Scripture testifies in verse 15, "Thou (Satan) was perfect in thy way."

Not only was he perfect in his way but, according to the 12th verse, he was the epitome of wisdom and beauty. Lucifer was, first of all, the wisest of all of God's created beings. God had established him as administrator of the affairs of the angelic realm. Although all authority resided in the throne of God, He had delegated certain administrative authorities to Lucifer. God had prepared him by creation for the discharge of those functions.

The Word of God reveals to us a number of functions that angels were designed to perform by the Creator. In Ephesians 1:21 we discover that there are different gradations or classes of angels. They are referred to as principalities, powers, mights and dominions. These four words refer to different gradations or classifications of angelic beings, each one with its own responsibilities, each one with its own sphere, each one with its own ministry.

Some angelic beings have a ministry of preservation. For instance, in Hebrews 1:14 the writer tells us that angels are min-

istering spirits; that is, they are servants who protect and preserve those who shall be heirs of salvation. If he could do so,
Satan would depopulate heaven by preventing people from receiving Christ as Saviour. He cannot do it because of the ministry of angels to those who shall be heirs of salvation. In Psalm
91:11 the Psalmist says that God will give his angels charge over
thee, to bear thee up in their hands, lest thou dash thy foot
against a stone. It comforts me to know that some of God's angels
waited through time until I was born, watched over me until I
could receive Christ as my Saviour, and continue to watch over
me now. When I drive the crowded freeways I'm thankful for
this scriptural teaching. Thus we see that innumerable hosts of
angels were created to watch over and preserve those who would
be heirs of salvation.

Some angels are the agents through whom God performs miracles. This is illustrated in Acts 5:19, where it is recorded that
the apostles were delivered from prison through the angel of
the Lord who opened the prison doors. This happened again in
Acts 12:7, 8. God brought release, but He worked through angels
to accomplish the miracle.

Then in Revelation 16:1 we discover that certain angels have a
ministry of judgment. We read there, "I heard a great voice out
of the temple saying to the seven angels, Go your ways, and
pour out the vials of the wrath of God upon the earth." As we
read through the book of the Revelation we notice that the judg-
ments of the end-times are administered through angels. We recall in Israel's past history, when God judged the Egyptians in
order that the Israelites might be delivered from bondage, it was
an angel that went through the land to smite the first-born son
where there was no covering blood. Angels then also have a ministry of judgment.

Then, in Hebrews 2:2 we discover that some angels have a
ministry of revelation as channels through which God's truth is
revealed to men. He says in that verse, "if the word spoken by
angels was steadfast, and every transgression and disobedience
received a just recompense of reward; how shall we escape . . . ?"
He perhaps is looking back to the experience at Mt. Sinai where

the law was delivered to Moses through the ministry of angels. That is another classification of work assigned to the angels.

The previous ministries, you will notice, all had to do with men. But other angels perform ministries having to do with God. In Isaiah 6:1 we find Isaiah says, "In the year that King Uzziah died I saw also the Lord sitting upon a throne, high and lifted up, and his train filled the temple. Above it stood the seraphim. . . ." Now the seraphim were a class of angels with a ministry that was Godward. These seraphim surrounded the throne of God and cried one to another, "Holy, holy, holy, is the Lord God of hosts: the whole earth is full of his glory." These angels are worshiping angels who protect the throne of God from any invasion by unholiness.

In the first chapter of the prophecy of Ezekiel, we find a reference again to angelic beings, referred to in verse 5 as "four living creatures." In verse 13 we find that they had an appearance like unto "burning coals of fire, like the appearance of lamps: it went up and down among the living creatures; and the fire was bright, and out of the fire went forth lightning. And the living creatures ran and returned as the appearance of a flash of lightning." You will notice the angels are referred to as "burning," as "shining" as "lamps" that are lit, or as "lightning." The word *seraphim* in Isaiah 6:2 means literally *shining ones,* or *burning ones.* Here in Ezekiel 1 the glow that emanated from these angelic beings is described.

In Ezekiel 10:1 these who were called "living creatures" in chapter 1 are called cherubim: "Then I looked, and, behold, in the firmament that was above the head of the cherubim there appeared over them as it were a sapphire stone, as the appearance of the likeness of a throne." Verse 3, "Now the cherubim stood on the right side of the house, when the man went in; and the cloud filled the inner court. Then the glory of the Lord went up from the cherub." In referring to the cherubim, the prophets are speaking of another class or gradation of angels who had a ministry before the throne of God different from the seraphim.

The cherubim occur several times in the Word of God. In Genesis 1:24, after the sin of Adam and Eve, God expelled them from the garden and placed a cherub with a fiery sword at the gate to keep the gate of the garden. The next reference to cherubim is in Exodus 25:18 where Moses was told to build an ark, the ark of the covenant, and there was to be a mercy seat built on that ark as the lid for the ark and two cherubim were to be placed on top of the ark and they surrounded the mercy seat. Then in Revelation 4 we find another reference to these living creatures, the cherubim, in verses 8 and 9. John says that these living creatures "rest not day and night, saying, Holy, holy, holy, Lord God Almighty, which was and is, and is to come. And . . . those beasts give glory and honour and thanks to him that sat on the throne, who liveth for ever and ever." You will notice that these living creatures in Revelation 4 are worshipers. As the seraphim cried "Holy, holy, holy, Lord God Almighty," they were looking out from the throne to protect it from any invasion by unholiness. When the cherubim surround the throne, they are looking toward the throne and declaring that the One who sits on the throne is "holy, holy, holy, Lord God Almighty." The cherubim in Genesis 3 at the gate of Eden were there to protect holiness. The cherubim were on the ark of the covenant over the mercy seat declaring that through the offering of blood holiness would be satisfied. The cherubim in Revelation are worshiping before God because Christ's victory over Satan has vindicated God's holiness.

When we turn back to Ezekiel 28:14 we discover that Lucifer was one of the anointed cherubs that covereth. Hence you can see from the preceding discussion Lucifer's exalted position at the time of his creation. Lucifer was not some angel of a lesser order. He was one of the cherubs that could look upon the throne of God and could voice praise and thanksgiving, adoration and worship to God because He was a holy God. Now if we were to try to assign positions to the different orders of angels, we would conclude that the cherubim who could stand and look Godward, or minister throneward occupied the highest position of all and had the greatest privilege of any created being. It was over such a privileged class of angels that Lucifer was placed in authority by Divine appointment.

Satan was not only the wisest of created beings, but also the most beautiful. In Ezekiel 28:13 the prophet describes for us something of the beauty of Lucifer. He does it by referring to him through the use of precious stones. He says, "Every precious stone was thy covering, the sardius (which is a reddish-brown stone), the topaz (golden yellow), the diamond (colorless, reflecting all colors), the beryl (which is a dark red stone), the onyx (which is multicolored), the jasper (which is bluish-green), the sapphire (which is deep rich blue), the emerald (with its scintillating green), the carbuncle (or garnet, which is deep blood-red)." What an array of color! What a rainbow of brilliance! But, of course, a gem stone has no light of its own. If you were to take any gem stone into a dark room, it would not shine. It would not glow. Its beauty is not in itself! Its beauty is in its ability to reflect light from without. When God created Lucifer, God created him with a capacity to reflect the glory of God to a greater degree than any other created being. All of the beauty that was seen in this highest of angelic beings was a beauty that was given to him by creation, not a beauty that was innately his own. It was a reflected beauty. God in His holiness was the light that made Lucifer radiate and scintillate the glory that was His. It could be said that Lucifer was perfect in beauty, for no creature so fully reflected the glory of God.

Musical instuments were originally designed to be means of praising and worshiping God. It was not necessary for Lucifer to learn to play a musical instrument in order to praise God. If you please, he had a built-in pipe organ, or, he was an organ. That's what the prophet meant when he said "the workmanship of thy tabrets and of thy pipes was prepared in thee in the day that thou was created." Lucifer, because of his beauty, did what a musical instrument would do in the hands of a skilled musician, bring forth a paeon of praise to the glory of God. Lucifer didn't have to look for someone to play the organ so that he could sing the doxology — he was a doxology. The very beauty of God reflected through Lucifer brought praise and honor and glory to God. Lucifer was called the shining one, the light bearer, and no other angel could reflect the degree of the glory of God that Lucifer reflected as he shone forth with praise to the God who had created him.

What is the responsibility of a creature? To be in subjection to his creator. The creature must recognize that he has come from the hand of God and that the Creator is superior over him. But we read in Ezekiel 28:16, 17 that Lucifer left the place of a creature and usurped the position of the Creator. "Thine heart was lifted up because of thy beauty, thou hast corrupted thy wisdom by reason of thy brightness." God, who had demonstrated the exceeding greatness of His power by building such beauty and glory into Lucifer, was not recognized by the creature as sovereign. The wisdom that God had given to Lucifer was perverted. He said in effect, "One as wise as I ought to be God; one as beautiful as I ought to be worshiped and not to worship another." And it was that which God had given to him that became the snare that perverted him from the place of obedience, the place of submission and the place of subjection. This one who was created to demonstrate and to manifest the glory of God sought to glorify himself through his declaration of independence. Did God know the pride that would captivate the heart of Lucifer when He created him? Yes, since God is omniscient, He knew. Could God have prevented it? Yes, because God is omnipotent, He could have. Why didn't He? No one knows. God has chosen to enter into conflict with the prince of the power of the air so that through His victory over the innumerable hosts of wickedness God can demonstrate to all of creation that He is a God of glory, a God of holiness, a God of power, a God who is worthy to be worshiped and praised.

Some years ago when I was a pastor in the Philadelphia area, a man came into our congregation who moved from the midwest to assume a position in the precious gem section of the large John Wanamaker store in Philadelphia. In calling on him several times in the course of pastoral ministry, I had talked to him about his work and about some of the gems that he had seen and handled. One day I was passing through the store and he beckoned to me and said, "I thought you might like to see a diamond that we just got in from an estate." He went back into the vault and came

out with a little chamois bag, and said, "Hold out your hand."
He opened the drawstring and shook a stone into my hand and
asked, "Have you ever held a half-a-million dollar diamond in
your hand before?" I said, "Not too often!" He had placed a
half-million dollar diamond into my palm. It made chills run
up and down my spine. When I examined the huge stone, I was
overwhelmed with disappointment because even the little stone
that my wife wore on her finger shone more brilliantly and had
a lot more life and fire than that diamond had. Evidently he
could read my mind. He smiled and said, "Let me have it." He
reached down under the counter and took out a piece of black
velvet and put the stone right in the middle. Suddenly that diamond just leaped into life. It was brilliant and sparkling. He explained that, when I held the diamond in my hand, because it
reflected the color of my flesh, it became very dead and dull.
But, when he put it on a black background, it reflected the light
and then we could see the diamond's beauty. Even so, when
God would show forth the perfection of His holiness, He revealed
it against the black backdrop of sin. When Jesus Christ came
to save sinners, the contrast between Himself and sinful humanity
made the glory of His absolute holiness shine.

I believe that no man can ever grasp why God permitted Satan
to fall. But Scripture records the fact that the wisest, the most
beautiful of God's created beings looked away from the Creator to
himself. He failed to recognize that all he was and all he had
came as a gracious bestowment from the hand of the Creator to
whom he was responsible. In turning away from God, he turned
to himself and became an essentially selfish being. Every man
born into this world from the time of Adam's sin has had a
nature just exactly like his father, the devil. That which characterizes sinful man is selfishness, self-centeredness. Man is characterized by pride. He lives his life in independence of God
and he is only perpetuating the nature of his father, the devil.
Unless you come to understand something of the basic selfishness,
pride and independence that characterized Satan when he left
his original state, you will neither understand yourself nor will
you understand the temptations that come day by day.

A man today may walk according to Lucifer's pattern. He may become proud of his education, of his intellectual capacities, of his attainments and not recognize that all that he has is a gift from God. He may become proud of all he has in the material realm and fail to recognize that it has come from God. He may become proud of his position in the professional world and not recognize that it too is God's gracious gift. When a man sees himself apart from God, then he is perpetuating the sin of Lucifer by walking according to his own way. A man's pattern that conforms to Lucifer may be broken — only when he receives Jesus Christ as a personal Saviour. He then, by a new birth, receives a new nature; his basic selfishness can give way to a concern for others. Pride that once characterized his every thought lets the newborn child of God see himself in relationship to God; he sees that he is nothing, that he is dependent upon a father. May God bring you to the place that you will recognize that you are a child of your father, the devil. You are not little Lucifers; you are little devils. There is a vast difference. It is God's desire to take you out of that family and bring you into His family. Will you accept Him as your Saviour?

2

The Sin of Satan

Isaiah 14:12 - 17

Lucifer, the wisest and most beautiful of all of God's created beings, had been placed in a position of authority over all the cherubs that surrounded the throne of God. It was the responsibility of the creature to be in subjection to the Creator and that which was true throughout the angelic realm was more than ever true of Lucifer, for privilege brings responsibility. The very things that set Lucifer apart from all the other angelic beings brought about his downfall. As we saw in our previous study in the 28th chapter of Ezekiel, Lucifer's heart was lifted up because of pride in his beauty, in his wisdom, in his privileges and responsibilities. Were it not for divine revelation we would forever be ignorant concerning the thought processes that produced Lucifer's rebellion against God. In Isaiah 14:12-14, God has seen fit to reveal to us, step by step, what went on in Satan's heart.

Five times in these verses we have the declaration coming from the heart of Satan, "I will." We see at the outset that a conflict came about between the will of God and the will of Lucifer. God did not create Lucifer as a fallen satanic being, a rebel against God, the enemy of all good, the enemy of God. When Lucifer was created, he was created to be in subjection to God. But he was created with a capacity to choose. When God revealed His purpose for Lucifer, it opened up the possibility that Lucifer might rebel against the plan and purpose of God. Sin began when he pitted his will against the will of God and said five times, "I will . . . I will . . . I will . . . I will . . . I will . . . . "

20

Each time he set his will against the will of God he was substituting his own purpose and program for the program of God. These five statements are significant because they reveal to us Satan's program. He has not changed his purpose, nor has he altered his will; he is still determined to pursue these five desires.

In Isaiah 14:13 we read: "Thou hast said in thine heart I will ascend into heaven, I will exalt my throne above the stars of God; I will sit also upon the mount of the congregation, in the sides of the north, I will ascend above the heights of the clouds, I will be like the most High." Let us consider these five "I wills" of Satan.

First of all, he said, "I will ascend into heaven." In the Scriptures the word *heaven* is used to refer to three different spheres. There is what we might refer to as the first heaven, in which the birds fly. It refers to the atmosphere that envelops this earth, that makes life possible upon this earth. The second heaven is interstellar space. The stars are in this heaven. The third heaven envelops all; is the abode of God Himself, the seat of God's sovereign authority, that place from which God manifests His rule over the interstellar heavens and the heavens that envelop this earth or the atmosphere.

Lucifer dwelt in the second heaven, the heaven of the interstellar spaces. He desired to ascend into the abode of God. Now his desire to ascend was not the desire of a tourist to go to visit to see what the throne of God was like, because Lucifer, who dwelt in the second heaven along with all the other created angels, already had access to the third heaven or access to the throne of God. In the sixth chapter of Isaiah and verse 1, we read: "In the year that King Uzziah died I saw also the Lord sitting upon a throne, high and lifted up, and his train filled the temple. Above it stood the seraphim: each one had six wings; with twain he covered his face, and with twain he covered his feet, and with twain he did fly. And one cried unto another, and said, Holy, holy, holy, is the Lord of hosts; the whole earth is full of his glory." In Isaiah's vision of the glory of God and His throne, the prophet saw the seraphim. You will recall from our previous study in the 28th chapter of Ezekiel, verse 14, the word written concerning Lucifer, "Thou art the anointed cherub that covereth." In verse 13, "Thou has been in Eden the garden of God." Again in verse 14, "thou wast upon the holy mountain of God; thou hast walked up and down in the midst of the stones of fire." And by his appointment Lucifer ministered before the very throne of God, in the abode of God, or in the third heaven.

So when Isaiah said in chapter 14 and verse 13, "Thou hast said in thine heart, I will ascend into heaven," Lucifer was not desiring to spend more time as one of the cherubim ministering before the throne of God. He who came there to minister by divine permission desired to abide there as God abode there eternally. He who came to the presence of God wanted to make himself equal with God. The creature desired to expel the Creator. The one who came into being by the word of God wanted to move God off His throne and occupy that throne as though it were rightfully his. So his first will was to pit himself against the will of God by saying, "I will ascend into heaven" to occupy the abode of God.

The second "I will" reads, "I will exalt my throne above the stars of God." In Job, chapter 38 and verse 7, we have a clue as to the meaning of the phrase, "the stars of God." Stars do not have life that respond to the will of God. Stars are inanimate objects. They do reflect the glory of God, as the Psalmist tells us, "The heavens declare the glory of God; and the firmament sheweth His handiwork." But the stars do not voluntarily submit to the authority of God. What then was in Satan's mind when he said, "I will exalt my throne above the stars of God"? In the 38th chapter of Job, Job is invited to consider the majesty and the power of God as it is seen in creation. In the seventh verse the question is asked, "Where were you when the morning stars sang together and all the sons of God shouted for joy?" The morning stars are equated with the sons of God. The "morning stars" called here *the sons of God* refer to the created angelic hosts that burst into a paeon of praise when they beheld the glory and power of God as they are demonstrated in God's creative work. So from Job 38 we would conclude that when Lucifer said, "I will exalt my throne above the stars of God," he was saying, "I will usurp God's authority over the entire angelic creation."

We know from the Word of God that angels are created beings in subjection to some authority above themselves, for a creature must be subject to authority. Lucifer, in the will of God, was appointed overseer over all the angelic beings. But Lucifer's authority was a delegated authority; the right to rule was God's. Even though God appointed him as administrator over all the angelic hosts yet he himself was subject to God, and while he might administer the affairs of angels yet he must be ruled by another. When Lucifer said, "I will exalt my throne above the stars of God," he was saying, "I will become the sole administrator of all the affairs of the angelic hosts without submitting myself to the authority of the Creator." When the angels looked to Lucifer for their orders, they recognized that he was receiving orders for them from another as one in the chain of command. He said, "I will become the absolute, the ultimate. I will originate all of the orders that are given unto angels and I will eliminate God from the scene." He wanted to receive the recognition that rightly belonged to God from the vast created angelic hosts. He not only wanted to occupy heaven; he wanted to administer the authority that belongs to God alone.

In his third "I will" he said, "I will sit also upon the mount of the congregation, in the sides of the north." In this statement Lucifer expressed a desire to control all the affairs of the universe. Turn with me to several passages that show us the Old Testament usage of this phrase "the mount of the congregation" or "the sides of the north." In Isaiah 2:2 we read, "And it shall come to pass in the last days, that the mountain of the Lord's house shall be established in the top of the mountains, and shall be exalted above the hills; and all nations shall flow unto it." Notice the terms "mountain and hills" used there. Mountain and hill refer to *authority* or the *right to rule*. They have to do with Messiah's authority as King on the earth. When He comes the second time, He will establish a throne. He will rule as a king in His Kingdom, called here a mountain, and all of the lesser nations that will be under His authority are referred to as hills. In Psalm 48:2, speaking of Jerusalem, the Psalmist says, "Beautiful for situation, the joy of the whole earth, is mount Zion, on the sides of the north, the city of the great King." And the "sides of the north" here refers to the authority that belonged to Jerusalem in David's kingdom. Jerusalem was the capital city, the seat of authority; it was where the king ruled and administered the affairs of his kingdom.

In the light of Isaiah 2 and Psalm 48, we realize that when Lucifer said, "I will sit upon the mount of the congregation, in the sides of the north," he was saying, "I want to administrate the affairs of this earth and the affairs of this entire created universe." So the one who said, "I want to move in and occupy heaven," and "I want to bring all the angels under my absolute authority," reached out in his desire for power and said, "I also want to bring the entire created universe under my sway and include it in my sphere of authority."

In the fourth place he said, "I will ascend above the heights of the clouds." Turn back to Exodus 16. We read there that as the children of Israel moved out of the land of Egypt and came into the wilderness they were moving with God. In Exodus 16:10 it is written, "It came to pass, as Aaron spake unto the whole congregation of the children of Israel, that they looked toward the wilderness, and, behold, the glory of the Lord appeared in the clouds." And the appearance of the cloud was a visible manifestation to Israel that God was present among them and that God was preceding them into the wilderness to prepare the way. In Exodus chapter 40, verse 33 we read that when Moses finished the work of building the tabernacle, then a cloud covered the tent of the congregation and the glory of the Lord filled the tabernacle. And the visible evidence to the nation Israel that God would appropriate and occupy the tabernacle was that God revealed His presence by the appearance of a cloud in the tabernacle. Again in I Kings 8:10, after Solomon had erected the magnificent temple, the sign that God would occupy and possess that temple was that God revealed His presence by a cloud. "And it came to pass, when the priests were come out of the holy place, that the cloud filled the house of the Lord." In the New Testament in Matthew 24:30 where Christ promised His second advent to the earth, He tells us that He will come in clouds with power and great glory. The cloud in both the Old Testament and in the New was a visible sign to the nation that God was personally present with them. The cloud was a cloud of beauty and glory.

When Lucifer said, "I will ascend above the heights of the clouds," he was saying, "I will take to myself a greater glory than belongs to God Himself." You will remember that Ezekiel described the beauty and the glory that belonged to Lucifer in terms of the sun shining on polished gems. But the glory that belonged to Lucifer was not inherently his; it was a reflected glory. For God, who is the author of glory, God, who is the all glorious One, revealed His glory through the work that came from His hand. Lucifer's desire was to occupy the throne of God, rule over the angelic realm, and rule over the entire universe so that he could add to the glory that was his as a creature all the glory that belonged to God as a Creator. How insane the thinking of this one that he could add glory to the infinite glory of God. It suggests that there was a deficiency in the glory of God and that Lucifer could complete that which was lacking. By appropriating all of God's infinite glory and adding that to the created glory that was his, Lucifer would be unique in the universe over which he had imposed his rule.

Then finally he said, "I will be like the most High." Lucifer would have had to have acknowledged the fact that he was a created being. As such he possessed a created kind of life, for he was not created possessing eternal life. He had a beginning. In what way then could a creature be like the Creator? In what way could he be like the most High? He was the wisest of God's beings but he was not omniscient; he did not know all things. He was the most powerful of all of God's created beings, but he was not omnipotent. He could go from one end of the created universe to another, but he was not omnipresent. In what way could he be like the most High? There was only one way. That was to be totally and completely independent of any authority outside of himself. He could be like God only in being responsible to no one but himself. The desire of Satan was to

move in and occupy the throne of God, exercise absolute independent authority over the angelic creation, bring the earth and
all the universe under his authority, cover himself with the glory
that belongs to God alone, and then be responsible to no one
but himself.

Now what generated such an insane, inconceivable lust for
power and glory as that? Again Ezekiel gives us the clue. You
may see it in Ezekiel 28:17. "Thine heart was lifted up [to set
your will against the will of God] because of thy beauty. Thou
hast corrupted thy wisdom by reason of thy brightness [or thy
glory]; Thou hast defiled thy sanctuaries by the multitude of
thine iniquities, by the iniquity of thy traffic; therefore will I
bring forth a fire from the midst of thee, it shall devour thee, and
I will bring thee to ashes upon the earth in the sight of all them
that behold thee." What did he mean when he said, "I will bring
forth a fire from the midst of thee"? The word *seraphim* used in
Isaiah chapter 6 means a burning one, a glowing one, a shining
one. God said, "I made thee by creation the most brilliant of all
my shining ones." A fire burned within Lucifer because of his
glory, because of his beauty, because of his authority. That which
was given unto him became a consuming, burning passion. This
burning passion to sit on God's throne, rule over angels and the
earth, bring the earth into subjection unto himself, cover himself
with God's glory and then exert his independence, led to his
rebellion and eventual destruction.

When Christ offered Himself as a Saviour to the nation Israel,
He began His presentation by sending messages to the religious
authorities of His day. He called on them first of all to repent, to
turn to God and receive righteousness from God. The leaders
began to question among themselves what it would mean for
them to repent and turn to God. Christ said to them, "I am the
light of the world. Come walk in my light." They realized that if
they acknowledged that Christ is the light of the world they
would also have to acknowledge that they were in darkness and
all the doctrine that they had taught was darkness. Christ said,
"I am the life of the world; come to me and receive life." They
realized that if they came and acknowledged that Jesus Christ

is the life of the world they would have to acknowledge that they who had professed to lead men in the living way had led men in the way of death. And the leaders in Israel rejected Christ and the offer of salvation that He presented to them. Why did they do it? Christ put His finger on the cause in John 8:44 when He said to these leaders who were turning the people from Christ, "Ye are of your father the devil, and the lusts of your father ye will do." Now what was Christ saying but that they were reproducing the sin of Lucifer? How so? Because of pride in their position, pride in their authority, pride in their intellectual attainments, pride in their professed knowledge of the Old Testament law, they would not acknowledge that they were wrong. He charged them with having deceived men, and they would rather reject Christ, the source of light and life, than to admit that their teaching was wrong. It was pride that congealed the Pharisees in their unbelief so that they were immovable.

The pride of Lucifer is being reproduced in unsaved men over and over and over again today. The unsaved man says, "If I acknowledge Jesus Christ as my Saviour, I'll have to admit that my righteousness is nothing. I'll have to admit that my intellect is not enough to discover divine truth, that my way is out of harmony with the way of God, that I am not sufficient to work out my own salvation." It is a humiliating thing for an educated, self-sufficient, independent individual to come to God and say, "I have sinned." It is the pride of your father the devil that keeps you from Jesus Christ.

Not only is Satan's sin reproduced by the unsaved, but it may be reproduced by the child of God as well. That is why the Apostle Paul writes in I Timothy 3:6 concerning those who are to be set aside as elders in the congregation. In giving the qualifications, he says that the elder should not be a novice, that is a new convert, a new believer. Why? "Lest being lifted up with pride he fall into the condemnation of the devil." The new believer may be severely tempted by Satan to think that he has been appointed to a position of responsibility because of what he is, because of the capacities that he has, because of the intellect that he has, because of the knowledge that he has, because of the example that he has set. He will reproduce the sin of Lucifer and he will declare himself independent of God. There is no child of God who is exempt from this temptation to reproduce the sin of pride, to renounce dependence upon God and submission to God, and, like Lucifer, to be independent of any authority outside of himself.

In Proverbs 16:18, the wisest man who ever lived, an astute student of human nature, wrote these words, "Pride goeth before destruction, and a haughty spirit before a fall. Better it is to be of an humble spirit with the lowly, than to divide the spoil with the proud." Pride goeth before destruction. In Romans 12, Paul gives us a catalog of virtues that will characterize the Christian who is controlled by the Spirit of God. The Apostle begins by saying in the third verse, "This I say, through the grace given unto me to every man that is among you, not to think of himself more highly than he ought to think; but to think soberly [that is in the true nature of things], according as God hath dealt to every man the measure of faith." Even when the Apostle outlines what is expected of members of the body of Christ, he has to begin by dealing with pride because we are so sorely tempted to reproduce that which burned within Lucifer, to declare ourselves independent of God.

It was said of Moses in Numbers 12:3 that he was the meekest man on the earth. Moses had more to be proud of than any man of his generation in Israel. He had been educated in Pharaoh's court. There is no question that his education was superior to that of any Israelite of his day. Moses could have been proud. He had a position exceeding any given to another Israelite because he was the official son and heir of Pharaoh's daughter. He had more wealth at his disposal; he had more power and influence and authority. And yet Moses was called the meekest man, not because he didn't have anything of which he could be proud but because of a divine work in his heart that prevented the temptation of Satan coming to fruition. Don't think that Moses wasn't tempted to be proud because of his education, his wealth, his influence, his power or his position. But he resisted the temptation. Moses was not used of God because of his education and his training and his ability. He was used of God because he did not succumb to the temptation of pride. He saw things in their true light. That is what sobriety is — seeing things in their true light. He recognized that it was not what he was, but what had been conferred upon him. In seeing things in the true light, he said, "I am nothing." There was a man that God could use.

If you are a person whom God uses day by day, it will not be because of how much you will know or what you have attained or how much you have. You will be used by the Spirit of God as you resist "the condemnation of the devil" or the sin of pride. You will recognize that all that you have comes from God and you will cast yourself in complete dependence upon Him. Then, and only then, are you a person whom God can use. I do not believe that there is any temptation that faces us more frequently or confronts us more persistently or entices us more subtly than the temptation to pride, because Satan is seeking to reproduce himself. Therefore let no man "think of himself more highly than he ought to think" lest we think like our adversary, the Devil.

3

The Hierarchy of Satan

Ephesians 6:10 - 17

Lucifer, the wisest and most beautiful of all God's created beings, was given the inestimable privilege of standing in the presence of God to oversee the hierarchies of created angelic beings. And the very thing that God had given to him by creation became the snare that brought about his downfall. Lifted up by pride because of his wisdom and his beauty, Lucifer desired to clothe himself with all of the glory that belonged to the Creator. To reach that desire, Satan lusted to move into heaven and occupy heaven as his dwelling place. He desired to rule over the angelic realm, and to extend his authority beyond the realm of angels throughout the universe. He desired to become independent of all external authority. If Satan is to exercise the power of God and the authority of God, then he must take over God's control over all created things and exercise that control into every realm.

We will consider first Satan's plan to rule in the angelic realm, and follow this with a study of Satan's plan to rule over the earthly realm to realize his desire to be like the Most High.

The average believer knows little about angels. We hold a tiny babe in our arms and look into that little face and, if perchance it is asleep, we address it as an angel. If it is awake and crying, we may call it something else. Because we have never seen an angel, we know little about their nature, about their activity, about their modes of existence, about their purpose. But the Word of God gives us a very clear revelation concerning this angelic realm. Before we can understand the realm of Satan,

30

it is necessary for us to understand some essential facts about angels.

In this materialistic world in which we evaluate something by its weight, size and shape, we give little place to angelic beings or the angelic creation. But the Word of God tells us that when God began His work of creation, that work commenced not in the physical realm nor in the earthly realm but in the angelic realm. Vast numbers of angels were created by the word of God. The Apostle Paul tells us in Colossians 1:16, "By Christ were all things created that are in heaven and that are in earth, visible and invisible, whether they be thrones or dominions, or principalities or powers, all things were created by him and for him." Speaking of the work of creation, the Apostle divides creation into two distinct spheres. There is the sphere of heaven in which invisible beings exist, and there is the realm of the earth in which visible beings exist. The one sphere is no less real because it is invisible. And the Apostle gathers together the total creative work of the Son and teaches us that the Son is the Creator of the angelic realm and the host of angels just as He is the Creator of the physical earth and those who dwell upon it. Angels then are created beings, created by the authority of God through the power of the Son.

Angels have personalities. Angels are not a force or a power, but are individuals who possess a personality. The Word of God refers to them as possessing all the capacities of personality. According to Psalm 148:2 the angels worship God. This is a volitional act showing us that they possess will. Angels worship God because they know God. They possess the capacity of knowledge. Angels worship God because they see that God is a God to be loved as well as to be obeyed and served. In Matthew 24:36 our Lord refers to the knowledge angels have or to certain things that angels may not know. In Scripture angels are viewed as beings who possess the capacities of personality, intellect, emotion and will, and are to be understood as individual beings with their own separate identity and existence.

Further, we discover in Hebrews 1:14 that angels were created to minister. They are referred to there by the Apostle as "ministering spirits who are sent forth to minister to those who shall be heirs of salvation." Angels are servants, and while there may be different ministries, angels as a class were created to administer the will of God, and God executes His will on the earth through angelic beings. Angels supervise the life of all men. They preserve those who are to be heirs of salvation. They are often instruments to bring divine judgment upon the earth. Angels, then, were created not to originate a plan but to execute a plan that was revealed to them by God who is the administrator, who has a sovereign will for all individuals who live upon the face of the earth.

Angels do not die. When our Lord's enemies came to Him during His earthly sojourn and sought to challenge Him on His teaching about resurrection, He told them in Matthew 22:28-30 that in the resurrection men are like angels for they neither marry nor give in marriage. What our Lord revealed there is the fact that the ranks of angels are not depleted by death so that it is not necessary to reproduce to keep the number of angels constant. Every angel who ever was created still lives.

Angels do not possess physical bodies but that does not mean they do not possess bodies. This is a mystery to many. Angels are conceived of as beings like a puff of smoke that float around and then dissipate and may reappear with no one specific point of existence. In teaching about the resurrection body in I Corinthians 15 Paul tells us that there are different kinds of bodies. There is a body that is suited to this earth. It is called an earthly or a terrestrial body. He tells us that there is also another kind of body that is a heavenly body or a celestial body. This is a body suited to the heavenlies, no less real than the earthly body.

We do not know the nature of the heavenly body, but we can learn a little something about the nature of a heavenly body by observing our Lord after His resurrection. It was a body that had form and shape and weight. It was not a body that was supported by the blood principle. It was supported by an entirely different principle for he referred to the fact that his body was now incorruptible. Our Lord's resurrected and glorified body was not limited by time and space. It could appear at one moment in Jerusalem and the next in Galilee. It was a body that could materialize in a room that was shut and sealed because of fear of the Jews. There are no natural laws to which we can refer that would explain how our Lord in a resurrection body could appear one place one moment and a hundred miles away the next moment, how he could appear in a room when all the doors and windows were shut and barred. But Scripture says that that was something characteristic of the resurrected glorified body.

Just as Christ had a celestial or heavenly body, angelic beings must have bodies not limited by time or space. This is illustrated in the ninth chapter of Daniel when God sent a message to Daniel. In verse 21 we read: "While I was speaking in prayer even the man Gabriel whom I had seen in the vision at the beginning, being caused to fly swiftly touched me about the time of the evening oblation." It was called to Daniel's attention that an angel can move from place to place with the speed of lightning. Angels were created to live in the heavenly sphere. They were not created to be earthlings, that is, to depend upon the existence of this atmosphere for life. Since no human body can exist outside of this earth's atmosphere, when our spacemen go into orbit, it is necessary for them to take along the earth's atmosphere to sustain them. Within the space capsule there is a miniature earth, the atmosphere of the earth. When they leave the capsule and walk around in space, within that spacesuit they still have by artificial means the atmosphere of the earth because the human body depends upon the atmosphere to sustain it. But angels were not created to dwell on this earth nor in this earth's atmosphere. They were created to live and exist in the sphere of the heavenlies. The words of our Lord emphasize this. In Mark 13:32 our Lord says, "Of the day and hour knoweth no man, neither the angels which are in heaven." And that phrase "which are in heaven" shows us the sphere in which angels exist and for which sphere they were created.

Since every individual has his own guardian angel, we would have to conclude that the number of angels must equal or exceed the total number of individuals who ever have lived or who ever will live on the face of the earth. The number of angels is no-where described in Scripture. They are simply referred to as being innumerable. We see something in the vast power of God who by one creative act could bring into existence such an innumerable host of angelic beings fitted to do the will of God, prepared as servants of God, to execute God's will.

Angelic beings are divided into many different ranks, and each rank has its own responsibility. This is referred to, for instance, in Colossians 1:16 where the angelic creation in heaven is divided into categories called thrones, dominions, principalities, and powers. These four words evidently represent different ranks or gradations of angels with their own responsibilities. *Thrones* would refer to angels who were created to sit on thrones and to rule. *Dominions* refer to those who exercise rule under God. *Principalities* refer to those who govern, and *powers* refer to those who exercise some particular assigned authority. When we examine the Word of God, we find that God has a system of governing His universe. God is sovereign and rules over all things, but God as an administrator delegates authority. We find, for instance, in Daniel 12:1 Michael is referred to as the "angel who standeth for Israel." God has created an angelic being to whom has been assigned a throne. He is, if I may use the word, the prime minister who exercises authority over a nation. The angel Michael is such an administrator over Israel, and Gabriel is associated with him. Thus God executes His will from His throne through angels who are assigned to thrones, to govern, to rule, to exercise power and exercise authority in a chain of command. I think it would be logical to conclude that, if Michael is the archangel who is prime minister for Israel, there were angels under him, twelve of them, who under Michael administered authority for the twelve tribes. There would be a further break-down, and under the leader of each one of the tribes would be other lesser ranks of angels to exercise authority over different areas in each tribe in Israel. What is true in Israel was also true for Persia, for in Daniel 10:13 reference is made to the "Prince of Persia." Thus a subdivided, administrative authority is vested in angels.

God, then, executes His will, and supervises the administration of His total universe through these ranks of angels who were created by God and who are in subjection to God. A common title used of God in the Old Testament is the title, *the Lord of hosts,* or "Lord of Sabaoth." And each time God is referred to as the Lord of hosts, He is the Lord of these created angels. He is not the Lord of the hosts of Israel; He is the Lord of the armies of heaven. God, before He prepared this earth as a place for human habitation, populated the heavenly sphere with innumerable created beings, each one with their own rank and their own station, and their own responsibility. Each one was to give worship and adoration and honor to the one who sat upon the throne. They acknowledged Him as the Lord of Sabaoth, the Lord of the armies of heaven. And God had but to indicate some manifestation of His will, and those angels leaped to obey and to execute that which was God's will.

When Lucifer rebelled against God and desired to usurp God's throne, before he could move God from His throne and rule as sovereign in this universe, it was necessary for him to bring angelic creation under his authority and control. In Revelation 12:4, we get a clue to the extent of Satan's original rebellion against God. For after telling us, in the third verse, that John beheld a wonder in heaven, the great red dragon, who is explained to us in verse 9 as Satan, we read in verse four: "his tail drew the third part of the stars of heaven." The stars there seem to refer to the angelic beings, and this seems to suggest to us that, at the time Satan rebelled against God, Satan started on a campaign to persuade the angels to rebel against God and to follow Him. And he was 33⅓% successful. For the angels who were created with the capacity of volition, who had the ability to make a choice, were confronted with a choice. They must either remain where they were placed by the Creator, or they must follow Satan with his promise that he would elevate them above what they were by God's creation. Lucifer purposed not only to elevate himself but also to elevate those who would follow him in order that they might rule with him over thrones and principalities and dominions and powers which he expected to subject to himself. And when Lucifer rebelled against God, he led away after him a third of the angelic creation, those who believed that Lucifer could serve the universe better than the Lord of hosts.

That group of angels which Satan led after him, he brought together into a kingdom like God's system. We will be bringing out in subsequent studies the fact that Lucifer has never originated any program other than his initial program to make himself superior to God. Satan is an imitator, not an originator; and when Satan rebelled against God and planned his kingdom, he patterned it after God's form of administration. We see this in Ephesians 6:12 where, referring to the warfare of the believer, the Apostle says "we wrestle not against flesh and blood but against principalities, against powers, against the rulers of the darkness of this world, against spiritual wickedness in high places." You will notice that Paul points out four different ranks in Ephesians 6:12 that are under the authority of Satan, and those four ranks that Satan has instituted correspond to the ranks mentioned in Colossians 1:16 that God had instituted in arranging the affairs of His universe. Satan has set certain of his followers on thrones giving to them authority. For instance, over Palestine there is one of Satan's minions who in Satan's governmental set-up corresponds to Michael, and under him a lesser one who parallels Gabriel, and under him lesser ones who have authority over the twelve tribes, and within each tribe those who have lesser authority serving under them. He has imitated completely the pattern and program of God in the administration of his affairs and the oversight of his kingdom.

These who followed Satan in his original rebellion we refer to as demons. These demons, these fallen angels, possess all of the capacity which they had before they followed Satan in his rebellion against God. All of the power, all of the wisdom that they had before the fall, they now possess after the fall. The demons are no more limited by time and space than angels are limited by time and space. The demons, while fewer in number than angels, are still referred to as innumerable, so there are vast hosts of fallen angelic beings. Satan is not omnipresent. He cannot be at your house and at my house at the same time personally. But that is slight comfort to me because one of his demons can be. Satan works, not through his own personal presence, but through those gradations of demons who rebelled with him and who have been assigned to responsibilities under him. The child of God is surrounded every moment of every day by these hosts of fallen angelic beings as well as by that guardian angel whom God has assigned to him. We are not dealing with an impersonal force; we are not dealing with a principle of evil as opposed to the principle of good. We are dealing with personalities, who have been assigned to frustrate and to defeat the will of God for us as God's children. They serve Satan faithfully, without interruption in their service. They don't punch in at eight and go home at four-thirty with a half-hour off for lunch and two coffee breaks a day, so that there are times when you are free from their activity because they are off the job. As spirit beings, possessed with spiritual bodies, they are not limited by space or by time. They can give constant attendance to you wherever you are and whatever you are doing. These who serve under the instrumentality of Satan dog your footsteps every moment just as constantly as God's angelic beings who execute the will of God faithfully stand beside you to preserve and keep you because you are an heir of salvation. Having once chosen to obey Satan, these demons obey him perfectly and completely. They persist in executing the will of Satan for you. And Satan's will for you is to defeat the will of God for you at any moment of your life.

We recognize that these demons have been assigned to their part in the lake of fire. Our Lord taught in Matthew 25:31 that the eternal lake of fire was prepared for the devil and his angels. They are assigned their part in the pit separated from God forever, under eternal condemnation and judgment. But while they are under condemnation, they are nonetheless active, and the frenzy of their activity seems to be motivated by their confident expectation of judgment to come. This is an awesome picture. But if we have brought to you this truth from the Word of God so as to make you conscious of your adversary, we will have prepared you for the victory that has been promised in Jesus Christ. When you blithely go on your way living from day to day as though you were separated from Satan's hosts you are not prepared for these satanic attacks. But when you realize that Satan after his fall organized his own kingdom so as to promote his purpose to dethrone God, you come to the consciousness that Satan is as concerned about watching over you as the Lord Jesus Christ is. If Satan is to defeat God's purpose, he has to do it in you and through you. Therefore, we are subject to these attacks daily, hourly, and momentarily. And since we are facing a foe we cannot see, and since we are up against an organized system of evil that seeks to dethrone God and to enthrone Satan, we must know his purposes. We must know his method of working in order that we might do what the Apostle exhorts us to do, "take the whole armor of God so that we may be able to stand in the evil day, and having done all to stand." Satan was not able to fulfill his will perfectly, and to draw all of the angels after him. But he did draw enough of them to organize an imitation system arranged after the pattern of God in order that he might fulfill his will to get the glory that belongs to the Lord of hosts, the Lord of the armies of heaven.

May I say to you, child of God, that every time you disobey God and succumb to the temptation of Satan, you are casting a vote for Satan instead of God? If you do not know Jesus Christ as your personal Saviour, may I say to you that you were born as a part of Satan's kingdom; you were born a rebel; you were born under his leadership, his headship. He is the god of this world, and you are following him as though you had no responsibility whatsoever to the God who created you. The only way you can come out from under his authority is to be born into a new family, to a new life. Christ died in order that He might translate us out of the kingdom of Satan and bring us into the kingdom of the Son of His love. If you accept Jesus Christ as your personal Saviour, God not only forgives you your sins, makes you His child, brings you into His family, but He breaks Satan's authority over you, and sets you free.

I offer you a Saviour who can liberate you from the kingdom of darkness and from the god of this world.

4

Satan's Conquest of the Earth

Genesis 3:1 - 7

As we discovered, Lucifer coveted for himself the glory that belonged to an infinite and eternal God. To attain that glory, Satan desired to bring an innumerable host of angels into subjection. In Revelation 12:4 we read that, when Satan rebelled against God, he led along with him a third of the created angelic beings. But Lucifer desired to clothe himself with the glory of God by also extending his authority into the earthly realm of creation. Then he might declare himself independent of God and claim an authority equal to God.

This desire to rule over the earth put a plan into operation. In the first chapter of the book of Genesis, at the time God created man, God said in verse 26: "Let us make man in our image and after our likeness, and let them have dominion over the fish of the sea, over the fowl of the air and over the cattle and over all the earth, and over every creeping thing that creepeth upon the earth. So God created man in his own image. In the image of God created he him, male and female created he them." And when God created man and placed man upon the earth, God gave man authority over the earth. Man was not independent of God. His dependence made him recognize that God was sovereign, that God had the right to rule, that God is a God of glory. But man was appointed as God's representative on earth in the administration of the things of God and God's kingdom. Man was a ruler, but he ruled by divine permission. Satan, in his desire to gain control over this earth, had to realize his purpose by attacking man.

When we turn to the third chapter of the book of Genesis, we find the first assault that Satan made in this earthly realm against God's representative, man. The record of the temptation is a very familiar one. Those who believe the Word of God believe that this was a literal incident, that it is not to be relegated to the realm of myth. This is not the personification of some vague idea that arose in the minds of men to explain the presence of sin that must be dismissed as a fact. This is history. Lucifer came into the Garden of Eden where God had placed man at the time of creation, in order to turn his heart away from the path of obedience to God.

When God placed Adam in the Garden of Eden, which was a reflection of the perfections of heaven, God said in Genesis 2:16: "Of every tree of the Garden thou mayest freely eat: But of the tree of the knowledge of good and evil thou shalt not eat of it: for in the day that thou eatest thereof, thou shalt surely die." This restricted the liberty and the freedom of man. Man is not free when he is totally independent of any authority. Man is truly free when he can choose the one whose slave he will become. And Adam was free in that he could choose to obey God, by submitting his will to the will of God. God had put this prohibition upon Adam: "Thou shalt not eat of the tree of the knowledge of good and evil: for in the day that thou eatest thereof, thou shalt surely die." It never entered into the heart or mind of Adam to question this restriction. It never crossed his mind to think that God had jealously withheld something from him that would have been for his good or his benefit. God in His infinite grace had provided for His creature all that he could want or need or desire. Yet when Lucifer came to test Adam, he tested him in the very area of God's prohibition, the area that had made Adam truly free.

We read in the first verse of Genesis 3 that the serpent was more subtle than any beast of the field which the Lord God had made. It should be observed at the outset of our understanding of Satan's methodology, that Satan cannot materialize his body which was suited for a heavenly existence so as to appear on the earth in physical form. If Satan is to manifest himself upon the earth in any visible form, he must appropriate a physical body through which to work. The eternal Son of God could appear in physical form. In the Old Testament the Angel of Jehovah is a preincarnate appearance of the Lord Jesus Christ on the earth. The Angel of Jehovah appeared in physical body and walked and talked with men. But Satan does not have this power. Rather, he has to operate by controlling a man or a woman or some beast of the field through which he can manifest his presence among men. When Satan came into the Garden of Eden to test Adam and Eve, to bend them to his own will, he chose to use the body of a serpent.

We are not to think that a reptile was originating this plan, that a reptile was contradicting the pronouncement of God, that a reptile was interested in the decisions which Adam and Eve made. This reptile only provided the body which Satan used. And it is recorded that the serpent (as now possessed by Satan) was more subtle than any beast of the field. For no animal ever yet has conceived the thought of rebelling against God. Animal creation is in perfect subjection to God. When Christ was tempted of Satan forty days in the wilderness, the gospels record that His only companions were the wild beasts. What is significant about that? Because all creation except man recognizes that God is sovereign. And the wild beasts that were with Jesus Christ in that time of temptation submitted to His authority. This serpent in Genesis was not chosen because it was wiser but because it was a suitable vehicle through which Satan could approach Eve. And it became wiser than any beast has ever been in that it advocated that Eve rebel against the will of God.

The subtlety in this approach was that Satan could approach Eve without revealing who he was or what his purpose actually was. For had Satan come to Eve and openly and forthrightly revealed himself as the enemy of God and had invited her to repudiate God's will, Satan could anticipate that Eve and Adam would have said no to him, repudiated his attempts, and his desire to rule this universe would have been thwarted. So it was necessary for Satan to change himself into something that he is not. If you turn to the New Testament in II Corinthians 11:13,

14, the Apostle notes Satan's use of this very method. We read: ". . . false apostles, deceitful workers [are] transforming themselves into the apostles of Christ. And no marvel; for Satan himself is transformed into an angel of light." This transformation is also referred to in the twelfth chapter of the book of the Revelation where, in speaking of Satan, we read in the ninth verse: "And the great dragon was cast out, that old serpent called the devil, and Satan, which deceiveth the whole world. . . ."

Now devil and Satan are significant words because they mean "deceiver" and "slanderer." When Satan came to oppose the will of God, he appeared as a deceiver and he slandered the character and the love of God in order that he might divert Adam and Eve from the will of God. Mark this principle: Satan always works by slandering the goodness and the holiness of God and by deceiving men concerning their relationship to God and the will of God. And the serpent by subtlety, by deceit, came with a question. "Yea, hath God said, Ye shall not eat of every tree of the garden?" This was a question to discover how much Eve actually knew about what God had said. If Satan is to deceive a man, he must start with the knowledge that the man has. That principle is true today. If a man is totally ignorant of the Word of God, so that he knows nothing of the person of God, of the character of God, of the requirements of God, it is easy for Satan to deceive a man into believing that he is completely acceptable to God without dealing with the sin question at all. But if a man knows the Word of God and the holiness of God, and he knows his own unholiness, then it is much more difficult for Satan to keep that man in darkness.

So Satan probed to find out how much of the Word of God Eve knew. Thus he raised the question, "Is it true that God said you shall not eat of every tree of the garden?" And Eve had to confess that God had put a restriction upon her for she said correctly: "We may eat of the fruit of the trees of the garden: but of the fruit of the tree which is in the midst of the garden, God hath said, Ye shall not eat of it, neither shall ye touch it lest ye die." You will notice that Eve knew the prohibition and she knew the penalty for disobedience. Now this much had been established: Eve was familiar with what God had said, that He demanded obedience to His word, and He had affixed a penalty for disobedience. On the basis of this knowledge Satan now proceeds.

Satan responded to Eve's knowledge with an outright denial. "The serpent said unto the woman, ye shall not surely die." This is a categorical denial of what God had said. And this is the greatest insult that any creature has ever offered to God, because he openly said God is a liar. He accused God of deception. Is it not significant that the one who came to deceive, the one whose nature it is to deceive should charge a holy, righteous God with that which is his own distorted and perverted character?

Then he explained in the fifth verse why God had withheld the fruit of this one tree from Adam and Eve. "God doth know that in the day ye eat thereof, then your eyes shall be opened, and ye shall be as gods, knowing good and evil." It is necessary for us to change the reading of this verse to discover Satan's intent. For the word translated "gods" is *Elohim* and it is an Old Testament name for God. Adam and Eve knew nothing of false deities. What Satan is saying is that, if you eat of this tree, you will be like God. Do you remember what the prophet Isaiah recorded as the desire of Satan? "I will be like the most High." Now his enticement to Eve was that, if she reached out and took of the fruit of that tree and ate it, in disobedience against God, she would elevate herself to the place that she would be just like the most High. Satan knew that the one who has the right to be obeyed has the right to be worshiped because he is sovereign. He also knew that, if he could entice Eve to disobey God, that disobedience would be an act of obedience to him and he, consequently, would have the right to be worshiped. And if man will obey Satan and worship him, he has usurped God's place in creation and he has become like the most High. He said in effect, "God is jealous; God wants to reserve the right to rule for Himself. He does not want to share His glory with another. God knows that, if you take this fruit and eat it, you will be elevated to His throne and you and God will be on an equality because

God has withheld from you the one thing that makes you less than God. And if you eat this fruit, you will be like God."

A desire was created in the mind of Eve to elevate herself to this position of equality with God, to clothe herself with the glory that was associated with the throne of God, a desire to share the glory of God's throne. And Eve reached out and took that fruit and ate it and offered it to Adam, and Adam ate it. And as a consequence, verse 7, "The eyes of them both were opened, and they knew that they were naked." They were naked, not in the sight of each other nor in the sight of the animals in the garden, nor even naked in the sight of Satan. They were naked in the sight of God because there is no covering for the disobedience that now characterized their life and their walk. There is no covering for the sin and wickedness generated by their rebellion against God.

To take that fruit Eve offered him, Adam had to release his hold on the scepter that God had given to him when He said, "Have dominion over the earth." For Adam could not hold the scepter and the forbidden fruit in his hand at the same time. Adam could rule only as long as he was obedient. And Lucifer was there to snatch up the scepter that Adam dropped.

When we turn to the second chapter of Ephesians, verse 2, the Apostle writes that "in time past ye walked according to the course of this world, ye walked according to the prince of the power of the air." That description, the prince of the power of the air, recognizes that Satan has usurped the power of God in the angelic realm. In II Corinthians 4:4, we find that Paul recognizes that Satan has usurped authority in another realm. "In whom the god of this world hath blinded the minds of them which believe not lest the light of the glorious gospel of Christ, who is the image of God, should shine unto them." Satan is called there the God of this world. In his rebellion against God, he led angels after him and became a prince in the heavenly realm. But by leading Adam and Eve into disobedience, he has become the god of this world. Satan by his usurpation of power in these two realms has sought to cover himself with the glory that belongs to God. As he is obeyed by an innumerable host of fallen angels,

he declares himself independent of God and equal or superior
to God. By the obedience given to him by all men from the time
of Adam's fall, Satan claims the authority that belonged to the
Creator, and that he now is sovereign in this earthly realm.

When we consider the temptation in the Garden of Eden,
we are impressed with the fact that Eve had a knowledge from
God. She knew the command of God. She knew the will of God.
She had been walking in harmony and fellowship with His love
in the garden in the cool of the day. Eve's sin began when she
substituted natural reasoning for divine knowledge. When she
listened to the whisperings of Satan who questioned the Word
of God, then she had taken the first step toward renouncing
the authority of God.

Doubt and skepticism have to begin in the mind. When a man
begins to approach the Word of God with his own natural mind,
he has opened the doorway to repudiation of the whole of divine
revelation, for he substitutes human reasoning for divine revelation. The Apostle points out to us in the first chapter of Romans
that the world does not know God. And the wisdom of God is
foreign to the wise men of this world. I Corinthians 1:18-25
makes this so clear:

> For the preaching of the cross is to them that perish foolish-
> ness; but unto us which are saved it is the power of God. For
> it is written, I will destroy the wisdom of the wise [that is all
> natural wisdom], and will bring to nothing the understanding
> of the prudent. Where is the wise? where is the scribe? where
> is the disputer of this world? hath not God made foolish the
> wisdom of this world? For after that in wisdom of God the
> world by wisdom knew not God, it pleased God by the foolish-
> ness of preaching to save them that believe. For the Jews require
> a sign, and the Greeks seek after wisdom: But we preach Christ
> crucified, unto the Jews a stumbling block, and unto the Greeks
> foolishness; But unto them which are called, both Jews and
> Greeks, Christ the power of God, and the wisdom of God. Be-
> cause the foolishness of God is wiser than men; and the weakness
> of God is stronger than men.

And when the Apostle came to Corinth he said, "I did not come
to Corinth as a philosopher because philosophy is natural reason-

ing, a natural, darkened mind seeking to reason its way into the things of God. I came as a revealer. I did not come to seek after light. I came to bring light. That light is in the Word of God. That light is in the Gospel of Jesus Christ." Therefore, Paul said, "I determined to know nothing among you save Jesus Christ and him crucified."

If one today trusts natural wisdom, natural reasoning, natural philosophy, he will never come to an understanding of the things of God or the person of God, because man by philosophy does not know God. One will not come to know Him until he sets aside his own wisdom and accepts God's revelation. Until one by an act of faith trusts that which is revealed in the Word of God, no matter how many degrees he may write after his name, he will remain in ignorance concerning the things of God.

Lucifer asked Eve: "How much do you really know?" His denial of that which she knew raised skepticism in her mind, and that skepticism produced disobedience. As as result of disobedience, the scepter that God had given to Adam was transferred to Satan. Because Eve was swayed by doubts concerning the truth of God, Satan clothed himself with the glory of God, because Eve and then Adam submitted to him and worshiped him instead of obeying God. You may reproduce that same sin. Until you commit yourself completely to the truth of the Word of God, make that the foundation for eternity and standard for your life today, you can be deluded and deceived and led in a path of darkness. Satan's desire is to keep you in his authority, to keep you under his control, to keep you subject to his rule. Not until you by faith accept Jesus Christ as your Saviour is there any deliverance from this kingdom of darkness, deliverance from the god of this world. Not until you receive Jesus Christ do you become a partner with God in eternal life. God offers you a Saviour who is the wisdom of God and the power of God and the righteousness of God, the One who can break Satan's rule over you.

5

Satan, the Deceiver

I Timothy 4:1 - 8

Lucifer, long before the creation of this world, coveted the glory, the authority, and the power of God. To take this glory to himself and to exercise this authority, it was necessary for him to lead astray created beings. God created beings who were to be subject to Him and glorify Him. Lucifer could not create. To reign as a god he had to lead astray those whom God had created. After Satan usurped authority in a portion of the angelic realm, he became the god of this world.

Satan is a deceiver. He has to operate in the realm of denial of the truth or in the realm of a lie. It was impossible for Lucifer to persuade the angelic hosts to follow him by telling them the truth that if they did so they would end up with him in the lake of fire separated from the Creator forever. When Satan came to Eve it was not possible for him to tempt her by saying that, if she obeyed him rather than God, she would join him and the fallen angels in the lake of fire forever. He had to lie. That is why, when our Lord was in conflict with the Pharisees who were rejecting the truth, He said in John 8:44, "Ye are of your father, the devil, and the lusts of your father ye will do." Christ said that these Pharisees were following a satanic system, that they were thinking just as Satan wanted them to think. He cited two of the characteristics of Satan that they were at that time reproducing: "Satan was a murderer from the beginning" and you are planning to murder Me. Then He also told these religious leaders, "Satan abode not in the truth because there is no truth in him. When he speaketh a lie, he speaketh of his own: for he is a liar, and the father of it."

In Revelation 12, John speaks of the work that Satan will perform in the tribulation period to defeat the purpose and the program of God. Then in the ninth verse of that chapter, John refers to the one whom he has pictured through the symbol of the great dragon and he says, that dragon was called "the Devil and Satan *which deceiveth the whole world.*" He deceived Eve into following him. As a consequence his deception has settled upon the minds and the hearts of all of Adam's descendants so that the whole world today is deceived. John has in mind that which is recorded in Genesis 3 where you will recall Satan questioned Eve's knowledge of God's word. When he discovered that Eve knew what God had revealed, he lied. He said to her, verse 4, "Ye shall not surely die." That was a categorical denial, for God had said, "Ye shall not eat of it for in the day that thou eatest thereof thou shalt surely die." The death to which He referred was the separation of the creature from the Creator, the separation of the soul from God. Physical death, the separation of soul from body, was pronounced as a result of that spiritual death.

God who is True had said, "Ye shall die." Lucifer (as the father of lies) was bold enough to approach Eve with his categorical denial and say, "God lied; you shall not die." Eve is now confronted with a decision, which one will she believe? When you have two exact opposites, both cannot be right. It was necessary for Eve to debate the issue. Did God lie when He said, "You shall die" or did Lucifer lie when he said, "You shall not die"? It was Eve's conclusion that God was the liar. That sounds so blasphemous we ought not even to think it, but that was Eve's decision: God is the liar and Satan is the true one. Because she believed the lie of Satan and counted God a liar she disobeyed God and partook of that forbidden fruit. She found out immediately that Satan was the liar because no sooner had she partaken of that fruit than she desired to bring her husband into her fallen estate. Together they recognized that God was true because they tried to cover up their nakedness in the sight of God by putting together fig leaves for a covering. This was evidence that they recognized and that they were now under condemnation because the word of God standeth sure.

When we turn into the New Testament we have the Apostle Paul's comment on this incident in I Timothy 2:14. "Adam was not deceived but the woman being deceived was in the transgression." Paul traces the sin of Eve to its ultimate source; she responded to a deception by the deceiver or, she responded to a lie by the liar.

This deceit is the characterization which the Word of God gives to us of Satan, and it gives us the first principle by which Satan operates. We want to emphasize this aspect of the truth. Until we realize that Satan cannot, under any circumstances, operate in the realm of truth, but must always operate in the realm of a lie, we will not be prepared for his manifestations or for the temptation which he presents to us.

The Word of God is very specific concerning some of the lies of Satan. Turn first to II Corinthians 4 for here the Apostle emphasizes the first area in which Satan lies, the area of the Word of God. Paul's authority is being questioned in the Corinthian church where there were those who despised his doctrine. They could not deny the truth of his doctrine. Therefore they denied that the Apostle Paul came to them with divine authority, with apostolic authority, and consequently with a message from God. They said he came with a message he had devised himself. To handle this objection the Apostle says in chapter 4, verse 1, "Therefore seeing we have this ministry, as we have received mercy, we faint not; but have renounced the hidden things of dishonesty. . . ." Will you notice that phrase? *We have renounced the hidden things of dishonesty,* or to paraphrase it, Paul says, "We have had no part in preaching and teaching a lie. We are not walking in craftiness." Craftiness suggests hypocrisy so that things do not appear as they actually are. That is *living a lie.* And next he says, "We are not those who handle the Word of God deceitfully." We have not lied when we presented to you the truth of God."

The Apostle is putting himself in contrast to these false teachers who have come in to deny the simple Gospel that a man is saved by faith in Jesus Christ. These false teachers had come in with their false doctrine. To propagate their false teaching they had said that Paul was a liar and lived a lie because he didn't believe what he preached. He claimed that his message came from God, but really he thought it up from his own philosophy. We are giving you the truth. But Paul said, "I was no liar and I was not dishonest and I did not handle the Word of God deceitfully but I declared it unto you as it is by a manifestation of the truth commending ourselves to every man's conscience in the sight of God."

If Satan is to hold the minds and hearts of men captive to his lie, it is necessary for him to blind men to the truth as it is revealed in the Word of God. The Word of God is Gods revelation given to us of Himself, and all that is necessary for us to know concerning God is revealed to us in the Word of God. Since this alone is God's truth, Satan must deceive men concerning the Word of God. If you were to study the history of doctrines from the time that God gave this Word to men to the present day you would find that the satanic attack against God is leveled first of all as an attack against the integrity, the authority and the divine inspiration of the Scriptures.

Men are openly repudiating the Word of God. Countless pastors stand in pulpits today, open a beautifully-bound copy of what they call the Holy Bible, but ignore its truths. They publicly repudiate the revelation of the Word of God and call themselves men of God as they are doing it. The Word of God, its integrity, its inerrancy, its authority is being attacked without apology in universities, in colleges, in high schools, in grade schools. It seems as though Satan has so conquered and controlled the thinking of this world, the learned, the wise, the educated and the educators, that only a small minority hold to the integrity and authority of the Scriptures.

That is a part of the satanic purpose and program — to propagate his lie that the Bible is not the Word of God, is not authoritative, is to be studied only as a curiosity of what men at one time thought about God, but it has no relevancy or relationship to our life today. We stand unequivocally for the absolute inerrancy and the authority of the Word of God. We believe that what God has written was written under the influence and inspiration of the Holy Spirit and is our rule and guide for faith and practice. Any departure from that doctrine of the Word of God is to fall into the lie of the devil. God deliver us from being subject to the deception that denies the authority of the Word of God.

Turn with me to I Timothy 4, a second area in which Satan propagates a lie, the area of the person and work of Jesus Christ. In I Timothy 4:1 Paul writes, "Now the Spirit speaketh expressly, that in the latter times some shall depart from the faith, giving heed to seducing spirits, and doctrines of devils." To paraphrase that to make it clear, Paul says, "They shall give heed to teachers who will seduce men away from the truth and to the doctrines that are propagated by the devil." The Apostle is anticipating just such a situation as that in which we find ourselves today. He predicts Satan will dominate the religious realm so that what is mouthed in the name of Christianity bears no resemblance to Biblical Christianity whatsoever, and that what is taught in Sunday schools and from pulpits in the name of God subtly and satanically denies the truth of the Word of God concerning the person and work of Jesus Christ. Now Paul says, "I want to warn you that there will come these teachers who will follow Satan's method of lying and seducing just as Eve was seduced and that Satan will be the one who is behind this kind of doctrine." You probably thought that when Satan came to a church he stopped at the front door and said, "This is no place for me." Oh, don't be deceived! For Satan has moved into the church and has planted his standards. He has moved into many pulpits and taken over control of the preaching and the ministry, subtly, cleverly but certainly, so that the truth of God is denied and blasphemed and ridiculed.

The Apostle John was anticipating this same thing for in I John 2:21, 22 John said, "I have not written unto you because ye know not the truth, but because ye know it, and that no lie is of the truth. Who is a liar but he that denieth that Jesus is the Christ? He is anti-christ that denieth the Father and the Son." You will notice that John has become very specific as to who is the liar. The liar is one who denies that Jesus Christ is the Messiah; the One who has come in the plan of God to redeem and to reign.

The same truth is taught in I John 4:1 where John says, "Beloved, believe not every spirit [that is every teacher who claims to come in the name of God] but try the spirits. . . . " You are to test the spirits whether they are of God. The test of any teacher who claims to be a man of God is to test him by the Word of God. The Bible is God's measuring stick. Try the teachers "whether they are of God because many false prophets are gone out into the world. Hereby know ye the Spirit of God: Every spirit that confesseth that Jesus Christ is come in the flesh is of God: and every spirit that confesseth not that Jesus Christ is come in the flesh is not of God: and this is that spirit of antichrist, whereof ye have heard that it should come. . . . " John says that a man's teaching concerning the person and work of Christ must conform to the Word of God, and, if he makes Jesus Christ any less than the absolute Son of God come in the flesh, he is of the devil and he is propagating lies. He has fallen for the deceit of Satan himself and is an instrument to deceive as well.

Satan is seeking to reproduce his character in his children. It is also God's purpose, as you so well know, to reproduce His character in His children. So here are two seeking to reproduce themselves. Every time Satan reproduces himself in you, it will be by a lie. Every time that God reproduces Himself in you, it will be through the truth. To make this very clear we observe through the New Testament that in the practical exhortations which the Apostles give to believers they have a great deal to say about the tongue. Why? Because the tongue is the instrument through which we so often give place to the devil. To put it bluntly, we lie. In Ephesians 4:29, the Apostle writes, "Let no corrupt communication proceed out of your mouth, but that which is good to the use of edifying, that it may minister grace unto the hearers." What is corrupt communication? It is a lie! In Colossians 4:6; we find, "Let your speech be always with grace, seasoned with salt, that ye may know how ye ought to answer every man." In Ephesians he says, "Don't lie." In Colossians 4 he says, "Tell the truth."

Although it seems so evident it scarcely needs to be empha-

sized, may we suggest to you that if Satan is to reproduce himself
in your life, he will begin by starting a practice of deception.
That propensity to stretch the truth to which we are all heir
is a satanic attempt to bring us into open and outright repudiation
of the truth of God. What fisherman is not tempted to add a few
inches to the length of the fish he caught? Or the golfer to slice
a few strokes off his score? Did you ever stop to think that that
is Satan trying to reproduce himself in you and make you a liar?
We lie and Satan's character is being reproduced in us. By nature
we're all braggarts. We like to impress people as to how much
we have done or what our accomplishments are, and we're never
content to tell the truth. We have to enlarge it, expand it, or
stretch it a little bit. We like to live a lie to impress people that
our income is a little more than it actually is. That is the devil
making a liar out of us. How often we conduct ourselves so that
our word cannot be trusted. We make appointments and don't
keep them. No word of explanation, no call to explain the delay
or an absence. That's lying and we are reproducing our father,
the devil.

How often we lie. Someone comes to us and says, "I have
such and such a need; will you remember me in prayer?" "Of
course, I'll remember you in prayer." It's a lie because you have
no intention of remembering them. Woven into the fabric of our
whole life is this temptation to deceive. We fall into the decep-
tions of the evil one day after day. Think of the excuse you gave
to someone on the telephone who wanted you to do something
you didn't want to do! Was the excuse you gave the truth or
were you making up a lie? When Satan gets his foot in the door
he can kick it open. Satan is a deceiver and although he perhaps
cannot take the truth of the Word of God away from you, he can
cause you to deny the truth. Thus, he can open up the citadel of
your life by this laxity of the tongue.

Another fact that Satan wants to deny is the truth that Jesus
Christ is the only way of salvation. There are myriads of men
who call themselves ministers of the Gospel who stand up and
preach a lie and don't tell men they have to accept Jesus Christ
as Saviour. They propose other ways. Mary Baker Patterson

Glover Eddy had another way. Joseph Smith had another way. Ellen G. White had another way. All the false cults that are abroad in the land are satanic denials of divine truth. They are lies of Satan to deceive men concerning the fact that salvation is by faith in Jesus Christ.

As a minister of the Gospel on the authority of the Word of God, I proclaim to you that Jesus Christ is the way, the truth and the life; salvation is by faith in Him and apart from Him there is no salvation. But by accepting God's gift there is total complete salvation. That is the truth of God. It is no lie. We offer you this One who could stand before men and say, "I and no other am the way; I and no other am the truth; I and no other am the life." We invite you to receive Him that you should no longer follow the lie of the devil but that you should know the truth as it is in Jesus Christ.

6

Satan, the Perverter

Isaiah 5:8 - 23

In dealing with some of the doctrinal and moral defections in the Corinthian church, the Apostle Paul wrote very bluntly that such conduct was dishonoring to the God who had redeemed them and to the Saviour who had died for them. In tracing the conduct to its ultimate source Paul shows that Satan is the author of discord, doubt, denial, confusion and every form of perversion. In II Corinthians 2:11 Paul stated that he was concerned "lest Satan should get advantage of us: for we are not ignorant of his devices." The Apostle Paul had had sufficient experience in dealing with our adversary to be able to detect his footprints whenever he came upon them. He knew Satan's philosophy, he knew Satan's purposes, he knew his method of working. He wrote to the Corinthians that he might impart to them what he had learned of Satan and his methods so that they should not be beguiled as Eve was deceived.

In a previous study we saw that Satan is a liar. We want to consider next the revelation of the Word of God that Satan is a perverter. He perverts or distorts that which has been given by God to man for his blessing and benefit. To pervert is to change something from its original or intended use. Back in the garden of Eden, Satan manifested to Eve not only the fact that he was a distorter of truth but also that he could pervert the program, the plan of God. He was characterized by this perversion.

In Genesis 3:5 when Lucifer came in the body of one of God's creatures to test Eve, he asked her if it were true that God had said that the creature should not eat of the tree of knowledge of good and evil. To this fact Eve consented. Then followed Satan's lie, his deception, "Ye shall not surely die." This lie was followed immediately by his first act of perversion. Satan said, "God doth know that in the day that ye do eat thereof then your eyes shall be opened and ye shall be as gods, knowing good and evil." What Satan said to Eve, in effect, was this: "God has not revealed the whole truth to you because God knows that as soon as you eat this fruit you will be equal to God, and God does not want anyone on an equality with Himself. So God has withheld this from you, not because it would be bad for you or harmful for you but because He is jealous and does not desire to share with you."

Satan distorted and perverted the whole purpose of God in demanding obedience from Adam and Eve. Through obedience man would continue in fellowship with Him. Through a voluntary submission to the will of God, God and man eternally might have fellowship together. Satan denied the truth and then distorted the use which God had intended in placing these restrictions upon the eating of the tree of knowledge of good and evil. We find that from this point on Satan has become a distorter and perverter.

There is no blessing, no benefit, no good gift that Satan may not and does not distort from the use which God intended. There is no gift of God which may not be perverted and distorted. For example, notice this comment concerning food. In Genesis 1:29 God said, "I have given you every herb bearing seed, which is upon the face of all the earth, and every tree, in the which is the fruit of a tree yielding seed; to you it shall be for meat [or for food]." Then in verse 16 of chapter 2, "the Lord God commanded man, saying, Of every tree of the garden thou mayest freely eat." This was the principle that God laid down in the garden: I have given it to you for food, there are no restrictions placed upon it; you may eat it freely. The emphasis in verse 16 is on the word *freely.* Thou mayest freely and unreservedly eat!

Now it would seem difficult to distort and divert something as simple as food to satanic ends but we find from the Scriptures that that is exactly what has happened. How does Satan do it? Turn to Colossians 2:21. Paul says that these Colossians are being brought into subjection to certain ordinances, ordinances concerning dietary matters, "touch not, taste not, handle not." The Colossians who have been saved are being brought under a law contradicting what God said in the garden of Eden. Whatever God has given to you for food *you may not eat*. A system was creeping into the Colossian church that would restrict the diet of these Colossians. These Gentiles were being brought under the law that was imposed by God upon the nation Israel. These are Gentiles who are exempted from any relationship to the Mosaic law but upon whom a law is being bound. Spirituality is judged by what man eats and doesn't eat. The Apostle says that the spiritual life of the assembly in Colosse is being corrupted because men are being subjected to a perversion of Satan.

We find the same thing in I Timothy 4:3, 4. False teachers had come into the assembly in Ephesus where Timothy was ministering. They were "forbidding to marry and commanding to abstain from meats, which God hath created to be received with thanksgiving of them which believe and know the truth. For every creature of God is good, and nothing to be refused if it be received with thanksgiving: For it is sanctified [set apart to God] by the Word of God and by prayer." Here was another perversion. This false teaching is called the doctrine of demons in chapter 4 and verse 1. What were the demons preaching? They were preaching that spirituality and the Christian life consist in observance of certain dietary laws, that if you want to be spiritual and mature, you may eat this and you may not eat that. Paul says that is a devilish doctrine. What was Satan doing? Perverting the good gift that God had given to His creatures.

But there is another way that Satan can pervert in this realm of food. In I Peter 4:3 we read, "For the time past of our life may suffice us to have wrought the will of the Gentiles, when we walked in lasciviousness, lusts, excess of wine, revellings, banquetings, and abominable idolatries." I am calling attention now to that portion of the verse that deals with the excess of food and wine. Now what had Satan done? He had made them gluttons, and by their gluttony they were perverting the intended use of food. Let us look at the commandment Moses gave back in Deuteronomy 21:20. The parents should say to the elders of their city, "This our son is stubborn and rebellious, he will not obey our voice; he is a glutton, and a drunkard. And all the men of his city shall stone him with stones, that he die: so shalt thou put evil away from among you. . . ." Do you realize that the sin of gluttony was as serious to God under the Mosaic law as was adultery, or murder? Solomon made a comment about this in giving instruction in Proverbs 23:1 and 2, "When thou sittest to eat with a ruler, consider diligently what is before thee: and put a knife to thy throat if thou be a man given to appetite." That is about as plain and blunt as it can get. He said it is better for you to slit your throat than to be fat. In the same chapter, verses 20 and 21: "Be not among winebibbers; among riotous eaters of flesh; For the drunkard and the glutton shall come to poverty; and drowsiness shall clothe a man with rags." In Philippians 3:19 Paul says in writing to the Philippians, "Whose end is destruction, whose God is their belly. . . ."

Now what are we saying? God at the time of creation gave food as a blessing to man so that his physical body might be sustained. But what use has Satan caused men to make of that blessing of God? He has perverted food from its intended use. Man now wrestles with the problems of obesity and, consequently, heart trouble and high blood pressure and all the rest that goes with overweight. Man rejects the life of grace and puts himself under legalism in respect to food, thus serving Satan's end. You can serve Satan at your Sunday dinner table as well as in a tavern on Saturday night.

Another blessing that God gave to man was the juice he put in that plump grape. It was there as one of God's blessings, but how Satan has taken that and perverted and distorted it and used it to accomplish his own purposes. That it was a blessing and a benefit is testified by the Apostle Paul himself who wrote to Timothy in I Timothy 5:23 where he said, "Drink no longer water but use a little wine for thy stomach's sake and thine oft infirmities." I do not believe it is difficult to detect what Timothy's oft infirmity as a traveling companion with the Apostle Paul was. He had plenty of stomach trouble, as every tourist finds out who tries to follow the steps of the Apostle Paul through Asia Minor. Paul says there is a good remedy for that. He says use wine medicinally, for the wine will take care of dysentery as few other medicines will do. Why was Timothy so concerned about this? Back in chapter 3 the Apostle laid down qualifications for elders and deacons. Paul said in chapter 3 and verse 3 that an elder must be one not given to wine. The strong inference here is that the elder must be a total abstainer. In giving qualifications for deacons he said again that the deacon must not be brought under the control of wine so that he is enslaved to it or dependent upon it. Timothy took these instructions and qualifications so to heart that he tried to live with the problem of dysentery rather than to use the medical means that were available to him lest someone should feel that he was faithless to the standards and qualifications for those who serve in the office of elder and deacon. Paul's concept was that what God had given could be a blessing and a benefit.

But how Paul's concept has been diverted, distorted and perverted among those who name the name of Christ as well as others! In our nation today the problems of alcoholism and the problems resulting from the sale and use of alcoholic beverages constitute, economically as well as socially, one of our greatest problems, but one we largely ignore for the sake of selfish indulgence and the tax dollar. And how often the child of God is not alert to the devices of Satan. We have grown accustomed to alcoholism for we have grown up in the midst of it and have adjusted and adapted to it. We do not realize that this is a subtle device of Satan who has taken another of God's benefits and blessings and perverted and distorted it to serve his own end.

That is why the Apostle has to write in Ephesians 5:15 to remind them not to depend on alcohol for their means of support but to depend on the Spirit of God. The one who does not want to walk by faith and trust the Holy Spirit of God to sustain him and take him through some difficult experience depends on his drink, on his cocktail to do what the Spirit of God was designed to do. The man who leans on alcohol to get himself through some trying situation will never learn to walk by faith and depend upon the Spirit of God. Do you think Lucifer wants you to walk by faith, to depend on the Spirit of God? How ridiculous! So how does he divert from a life of faith? He substitutes another of God's blessings and benefits and says, "Use alcohol to strengthen you instead of following the God-designed way of dependence upon the Spirit of God for your strength." That is his perversion.

What about the moral climate in which we find ourselves? Again we see the perversion of Satan. This so-called new morality or libertinism in the area of sex illustrates again the way by which Satan operates. The Apostle Paul said that the divine answer to the physical needs of a man and a woman was to have a husband or a wife. In I Corinthians 7 the Apostle made it very clear that the marriage relationship was God's answer to sexual desires. That which God has given as His greatest blessing to the human race has been diverted and distorted and turned to Satanic ends. The Apostle writes of this so clearly in Romans 1:25ff. "Who changed the truth of God into a lie, and worshipped and served the creature more than the Creator, who is blessed forever. Amen. For this cause God gave them up unto vile affections: for even their women did change the natural use into that which is against nature: And likewise also the men, leaving the natural use of the woman, burned in their lust one toward another; men with men working that which is unseemly, and receiving in themselves that recompense of their error which was meet."

This whole area of perversion, of immorality and promiscuity, is open evidence that Satan is a perverter of those appetites and desires which God has given for the blessing and benefit of the human race. Possessing them, perverting them and diverting them from their intended use, he produces all manner of uncleanness, immorality and impurity. The Apostle has to deal with this in epistle after epistle. He emphasizes the law regarding marriage lest husband or wife be unfaithful to each other. He deals with premarital sex lest young people follow Satan's path into premarital relationships which the Scripture forbids as fornication. The Apostle has to deal with it as he does in I Corinthians

7, as our Lord does in Matthew 19, concerning the problem of divorce, for divorce is a perversion by Satan of a blessing that God has given to the human race.

These are just illustrations that could be amplified many times over of the blessings that we recognize are God's gifts and yet which have been possessed by Satan and used for his ends. Satan will pervert any gift God gives: physical processes, intellectual ability, social heritage, material wealth. All may become his tools.

Not only in these physical things does Satan pervert and distort. In the realm of the relationship of the child of God to the will of God, we find that Satan operates, diverting an individual from the will of God to serve his own ends. Certainly the illustration of Jonah comes to mind. God revealed to that prophet, who by a lifetime of ministry had honored and served God, that it was His will that Jonah should go to Gentiles and preach the message of judgment to them. Jonah turned his back on the will of God and went down to Joppa and got in a boat to go as far away from the place to which God had sent him to preach as was possible. Why was Jonah doing it? He reveals why in the fourth chapter of Jonah. He knew that God would bring blessing through his preaching. He knew that God would grant repentance and confession and that God's judgment would be lifted on these Gentiles if he preached. To Jonah the blessing of Gentiles was displeasing. He wanted to see Gentiles judged; he did not want to see them blessed. Here Satan was operating to say to Jonah, in effect, "God is asking you to do too much. God is asking you to give up too much. Why do you do it?" Satan perverted and distorted the will of God until Jonah elected to follow the perversion that Satan had put before him.

We find this same attitude revealed in Luke chapter 9. There we find that our Lord, in verses 23 to 26, put a choice before those who called themselves his disciples. Jesus said, "If any man will come after me, let him deny himself, and take up his cross daily, and follow me. For whosoever will save his life shall lose it: but whosoever will lose his life for my sake, the same shall save it." They had to make a choice: whether they would be disciples of Christ or the disciples of the Pharisees; whether they would receive Christ or reject Christ. Then as you drop down in the chapter to verse 57 it is recorded that there were some individuals who came to Christ. One said, "I will follow You wherever You go." Our Lord reminded him that He didn't have as much as the birds or the foxes have; He had no place of refuge. That man turned and went away because it cost too much to follow Christ. Another said, "I'll follow You but let me go and bury my father." Now the father was still alive. But if Christ had no means of supporting His disciples it seemed good for this man to wait until he came into his inheritance. After his father has died and he has his own independent means of income then he could come and follow Christ. It would not cost him anything then. But he turned away when Christ said, "You must follow Me now." The will of Christ cost him too much. Another came and said, "Let me go and bid farewell to them that are at my home," and Christ rejected him. This one was bound by earthly ties to material things. You remember in Luke 14 one gave the excuse that he had just bought some property and had to look at it. Another said that he had bought some oxen and had to try them. And another said that he had married a wife.

Would-be "followers" could make up all manner of excuses. Why? Because Satan was perverting and distorting the will of God by suggesting to these men that if they followed Christ they would have to give up every material thing and He would not give them anything. He suggested they should accumulate material things for their ease and comfort and then they could consider what they should do for Him. It was a perversion and distortion of the will of God for these individuals. Certainly the rich young ruler comes into this class because he came to ask Christ to answer the question that was uppermost in his mind, how he could find eternal life. The young man was trusting his riches because he was very rich. Christ said that the man must cease trusting his riches, give away all that he had, and come and follow Him. The man went away because he was very rich; sorrow possessed his heart because his riches stood between him and the Lord.

What we are suggesting to you from these considerations is that Satan will come to an individual and will say that if you put Christ first in your life, you will lose. He says to a business man that if he runs his business on Christian principles, his competitors will win out and, if he is strictly honest in running his business, he will lose. That is Satan's suggestion; the will of God is too expensive. How many there are who have been confronted with what Jesus Christ demands of a man in complete conformity and submission to Him and have turned away because it costs too much? They have followed the perversion of Satan.

There is another area in which Satan perverts. He perverts the standards of God's holiness. This was the point of the lesson in the fifth chapter of the prophecy of Isaiah. It is summarized in verse 20, "Woe unto them that call evil good, and good evil; that put darkness for light, and light for darkness; that put bitter for sweet, and sweet for bitter." We are living today in the midst of a double standard of morals and ethics. The one standard is the standard of the Word of God that is a reflection of the holiness of the character of God. This Book reveals God and what God expects of one who walks with Him. God has one system and one standard of morals and ethics and conduct. Satan has perverted those standards so that this world's standard of what is acceptable conduct does not conform to the Word of God. Men call good evil and they call evil good. They have adopted the philosophy that the end justifies the means. Our nation is being shaken today by the so-called credibility gap. Some who have been elected to high office have adopted Satan's double standard. This goes not only in the area of politics but in every other area as well. Men call good evil and evil good because Satan is a perverter.

A final area in which Satan perverts and distorts is in the way of salvation. God has one standard. A person must be made as righteous as God is righteous before he can see God face to face. God offers a Saviour to the world. Christ could say of Himself, "I [and no other] am the way, the truth and the life." Satan distorts and perverts this simple truth and offers us a multitude of philosophies and doctrines that are all denials of the person and work of Jesus Christ. Multitudes of men and women are destined for a Christless eternity — they are headed for hell — because Satan is a distorter and a perverter and he has convinced them that one does not need Jesus Christ for salvation. With all zeal and energy they are giving themselves to the pursuit of salvation through some satanic perversion and deception, not knowing that the end is separation from God forever.

It is necessary for believers to know the devices of Satan so as to be on guard against his wiles. He who is the deceiver will pervert and distort every blessing that God has provided for you as His child. What the Apostle desired the Corinthians to understand in I Corinthians 12 - 14 was that, when they received any gift from God, it was necessary to make certain that that gift was being used under control of God rather than Satan. No gift we can think of has been exempted from this possibility of perversion by Satan. No matter how good a thing may be in itself, Satan can move in to pervert it, to distort it, to destroy it — if we permit him to do so. God give us the grace to perceive and prevent the work of the perverter.

7

Satan, the Imitator

II Corinthians 11:1 - 15

Satan is a liar and a deceiver. According to the eleventh chapter of II Corinthians, verses 13 to 15, Satan is also an *imitator.* In the third chapter of Genesis it is recorded that Satan said to Eve: "In the day that thou shalt eat thereof, thou shalt be like God [Elohim]." It was Satan's avowed purpose, not to make Eve as ungodly as possible, but make her as godlike as possible *without God.* And Satan's plan and Satan's program has always been to imitate God, to deceive men concerning his plan so that as they follow his imitation they will be convinced they are following God.

In II Corinthians 11:13-15 the Apostle Paul writes: "For such are false apostles, deceitful workers, transforming themselves into the apostles of Christ." Note that phrase, "transforming themselves into apostles of Christ." "And no marvel for Satan himself is transformed into an angel of light; therefore, it is no great thing if his ministers also be transformed as the ministers of righteousness whose end shall be according to their works." When Paul writes to Timothy in I Timothy 6:16, speaking of the eternal God, the blessed and only potentate, the King of kings, and the Lord of lords, who only hath immortality, Paul adds these words: "Dwelling in light which no man can approach into, whom no man hath seen nor can see." The Word of God makes it clear that no man has been able to look upon the unveiled face of the eternal God. Paul states it as a categorical truth that God dwelleth in light which no man can approach unto, that God is one whom no man hath seen nor can see. When Moses asked to look upon the face of God, God reminded Moses, (as it is recorded in Exodus 33) that no man could see His face and live. But God said that He would hide Himself in a cleft of the rock and He would cover Moses with His hand; and He would take away His hand and Moses would see His outshining, His effulgence, His glory, even though Moses could not see God's face. Moses beheld the glory of God and came away completely satisfied.

Based on this principle, we would conclude that, when Adam and Eve walked with God in the garden in the cool of the day, as it is recorded in the opening chapters of Genesis, Adam and Eve conversed with a God who was clothed with light. They knew of God's presence in their midst in the garden because of the outshining of His glory. On later occasions the same thing was true in the tabernacle and in the temple. The nation Israel knew that God dwelt in their midst because they beheld His glory shining in the pillar of cloud or the pillar of fire in the tabernacle and in the temple. The three on the Mount of Transfiguration knew that God was in Christ and was revealing Himself through Christ, for they beheld His glory, "the glory as of the only begotten of the Father, full of grace and truth."

God came to Adam and Eve clothed in light, and they rejoiced in His presence in sweet and intimate fellowship. God spoke to them out of the glory that surrounded His person. His voice became a familiar voice as they communed with Him. But the time came when Eve was approached by another blaze of light, a manifestation of glory, and, the voice that spoke this time out of the glory was somewhat different than she was accustomed to. This is evidently what Paul had in mind when in II Corinthians 11:14 he said: "Satan himself is transformed into an angel of light." It is our conclusion that the Apostle is telling us the form in which Satan came to Eve. He did not come through the naked body of a beast of the field. He appropriated that body and then veiled it in a blaze of glory so that it would appear to Eve that God had come again into the garden to speak with them. Eve was not suspicious at the approach being made by this serpent because the serpent and Satan who occupied that serpent were hidden away in a veil of light. Thus he appeared to Eve. And Eve, accustomed to approaching the light to hear the voice of God and to receive instructions concerning His will and His way, to enjoy fellowship with Him, once again approached the light. The voice this time contradicted what had been revealed previously, as the voice out of the light commanded her to take and eat so that she might be like Elohim, like God. It was the presence of the light that convinced Eve that it was God who was commanding her to eat. Satan deceived Eve because he had imitated the mode of revelation through which God communicated with His creatures in the garden. He appeared as an angel of light.

It never seems to have entered Eve's mind that God could not and would not contradict Himself; and that God who just had said that "in the day that thou eatest thereof thou shalt die" would not change and now say, "thou shalt not die, take and eat and you will be like God." Eve's mind was deceived by the one who transformed himself into an angel of light. But Satan, who hid himself by imitating God in the garden uses the same identical means of deception to perpetrate his lies today. Satan is still transforming himself into an angel of light, and Satan's representatives, his ministers, are also being transformed as ministers of righteousness (II Corinthians 11:15). While propagating that which brings death and darkness to the mind and heart of the sinner, they profess to be representatives of the God who is light and claim to be propagating doctrines that come from the God of light, the living God. This is a part of Satanic deception, the Satanic system that imitates the program of God.

We can illustrate this from several incidents recorded in the Word of God. You remember that, when Moses was sent to Pharaoh to tell Pharaoh to let God's people go, Moses questioned how he could convince Pharaoh since he could not convince the people of Israel. "Who shall I say sent me?" And God revealed His name, "I am that I am," the Eternal Existing One. He has sent you. But Moses, anticipating the hardness of the heathen heart, asked how they would believe him and be willing to follow him? Thus God gave to Moses the authority to work miracles and signs so as to authenticate his mission, his person and his message. We read in Exodus 7:11, 12, that, after Moses had performed his first miracle, turning the rod into a serpent, then Pharaoh called the wise men and the sorcerers. ". . . now the magicians of Egypt, they also did in like manner with their enchantments. For they cast down every man his rod, and they became serpents. . . ." And again in verse 22, the program is imitated: "The magicians of Egypt did so with their enchantments." Will you notice what has happened? God sent a messenger to bring deliverance and freedom to the children of Israel. He authenticated his message with miracles and signs. But Satan had his ministers, his sorcerers, his enchanters, who imitated Moses' miracles, with the result that through this Satanic imitation, Pharaoh's heart was hardened, "so that he did not let the children of Israel go." He set his heart against Moses and against God. Thus Satan imitated the miracles to deceive Pharaoh and the Egyptians.

We find another example in the experience of Paul. The Apostle was sent to propagate the Gospel of the grace of God throughout the Gentile world. When Paul started on his first missionary journey he went into Paphos. ". . . they found a certain sorcerer, a false prophet, a Jew, whose name was Bar-jesus, which was with the deputy of the country, Sergius Paulus, a prudent man; who called for Barnabas and Saul, and desired to hear the Word of God. But Elymas, the sorcerer, withstood them, seeking to turn away the deputy from the faith" (Acts 13:6 - 8). Now, what happened? Paul came to a man whose heart was hungry and crying out for a knowledge of God. He introduced this man to the Gospel of the grace of God. But Satan had his minister, who professed to be a minister of righteousness, there to tell this burdened sinner that this was not truth, that it was a lie.

This principle is further illustrated in the thirteenth chapter of the book of the Revelation. When the Beast is set up as the object of worship during the tribulation period, that one who ministers to the Beast, the False Prophet ". . . doeth great wonders, so that he maketh fire come down from heaven on the earth in the sight of men, [imitates the miracles of Elijah], and deceiveth them that dwell on the earth by the means of those miracles which he had power to do in the sight of the beast; saying to them that dwell on the earth, that they should make an image to the beast, which had the wound by a sword, and did live. And he hath power to give life unto the image of the beast, that the image of the beast should both speak, and cause that as many as would not worship the image of the beast should be killed" (Revelation 13:13-15). When God sends His two witnesses to pronounce judgment upon Jerusalem and invite men to wash their robes to make them white in the blood of the lamb (Revelation 11:3-12), Satan has one whom he transforms into a minister of righteousness to imitate the miracles of God, the miracles of Elijah, the miracles of Moses, to convince the world that what he is saying to them is truth. God sent men with authority to proclaim a message; and authenticated that authority by miracles. But Satan as an imitator sent his representative to perform the same miracles to deceive the minds of men and to turn them away from the truth.

We notice another area in which Satan imitates. In Acts 1:8 God said to the Apostles, "Ye shall be witnesses unto me, both in Jerusalem, and in all Judaea, and in Samaria, and unto the uttermost part of the earth." You shall be witnesses unto me! As you read through the book of Acts you find the Apostles spreading out all over the face of the earth to proclaim a Person; to tell men the Gospel of the good news that Christ died for our sins. The message that the Apostles brought centered in the person and work of Jesus Christ. They knew nothing except Jesus Christ and Him crucified. But as Satan saw the purpose and program of God to send men out to witness to Jesus Christ, he sent out his men to deny that one central truth. Notice several references to this in the eleventh chapter of II Corinthians. In verse 3, Paul says to the Corinthians, "But I fear, lest by any means, as the serpent beguiled Eve through his subtilty, so your minds should be corrupted from the simplicity that is in Christ. For if he that cometh [now notice these words] preacheth another Jesus, whom we have not preached, or if ye receive another spirit, which ye have not received, or another gospel, which ye have not accepted, ye might well bear with him." He preaches another Jesus by the power of another spirit that results in another gospel. This same thing is anticipated in I Timothy 4 where Paul says, "the Spirit speaketh expressly, that in the latter times some shall depart from the faith, giving heed to seducing spirits [or seductive teachers], and the doctrines of demons." Now this is not doctrines *about* demons; it is doctrines that demons preach in imitation of the truth concerning the person and work of Jesus Christ.

The devil is a preacher — don't forget it. He is diabolical in his preaching but he is a preacher, and he has another gospel and another Jesus and another power to perform that which he desires in the lives of men. And his demons are preaching actively. In I John 4:1, John taught the same thing. He says, "Believe not every spirit [or teacher] but try the spirits, [measure them according to the Word of God. And this is the reason] whether they are of God: because many false prophets are gone out into the world. Hereby know ye the Spirit of God: Every spirit [or teacher] that confesseth that Jesus Christ is come in the flesh is of God: And every spirit that confesseth not that Jesus Christ is come in the flesh is not of God: and this is that spirit of antichrist, whereof ye have heard that it should come; and even now already is it in the world."

Back in chapter 2, verse 22, John makes the same statement. "Who is a liar but he that denieth that Jesus is the Christ? He is antichrist, that denieth the Father and the Son. Whosoever denieth the Son, the same hath not the Father." Now Paul and John were anticipating the Satanic movement that would thrust preachers out into the world with a doctrine that denied the person and the work of Jesus Christ. Satan is willing to concede any other doctrine that you insist on believing, but he cannot and will not, under any circumstances, consent to have the death and resurrection of the Lord Jesus Christ preached to men. For the person and work of Christ is the heart of the Gospel. Therefore, Paul and John warned the church of the advent of these men who would come with another gospel, preaching another Christ, by another spirit.

Now what is the significant fact to observe? That God's method of reaching men is to preach; God's method of reaching men is to have men herald forth the truth concerning Jesus Christ. And Satan has not devised another program. He imitates the program of God and he sends his ministers, whom he claims to be ministers of righteousness, into the world to do what the saints of God are commanded to do, to preach. But going with another gospel by Satanic power rather than by the power of the Holy Spirit, they go out to deceive, to delude, to take away the truth from the minds of men as they propagate a lie. This is the plan of the imitator of God.

Paul emphasizes this as he writes to the Galatians. In Galatians 1:6-9, he says, "I marvel that ye are so soon removed from him that called you into the grace of God unto another gospel: which is not another; but there be some that trouble you, and would pervert the gospel of Christ. But though we, or an angel from heaven, preach any other gospel unto you than that which we have preached unto you, let him be accursed. As we said before, so say I now again, If any man preach any other gospel unto you than that ye have received, let him be accursed." The Greek language knows no stronger word than the Apostle used here on two occasions (verse 8 and verse 9) when he said that the one who perverts the doctrine of the gospel of the person and the work of Jesus Christ should be damned forever. Paul, understanding the devices of Satan, knew that he would imitate the program of God and deceive men by imitating God's commandment to preach throughout the world.

We need to be aware of a general misunderstanding. Looking at a gutter-bum, a derelict on skid row, we say, "Look at what Satan has done. There is Satan's masterpiece." I beg to differ with you. Satan is as nauseated and disgusted by that product as you are. Satan wants to wash his hands of that bum and have nothing to do with him, even though he belongs to him. Satan's masterpiece is the good, upright, honest, honorable, respected individual in the community who feels that he does not need Jesus Christ, he does not need God, that he can work out his own salvation without God's help. The man concerning whose character there is no question, against whose reputation there is no flaw but who leaves God out of his life is Satan's delight. That is Satan's masterpiece. Satan is trying to make his children as much like God as it is possible for them to be without their ever putting faith in the Lord Jesus Christ as a personal Saviour.

Satan is striving for perfection. He is seeking to produce a perfect man apart from Christ. Then he can say, "You are like God; by following me you have become like God." What is the goal of evolution? By natural processes and by control of environment and heredity, to produce a perfect specimen of humanity. Man is viewed as moving toward perfection by his own effort apart from the help of divine grace. Evolution is the theory that Satan propagates in order to accomplish his designed end of making men think they are as much like God without any actual knowledge of God or relationship to him whatsoever.

We read recently of a Satanic wedding in California, complete with a bride dressed in scarlet. On the altar was the body of a nude woman, symbolizing devotion to indulgence rather than to abstinence. The two individuals came together to be married by Satan. The distinguishing feature of this new Satanic religion is that it has no concept of sin; hence, it evokes no guilt. The founder of this religion is writing a new bible that will be a Satanic bible. Who is not shocked by the report? Do you think that Satan is proud of this? No. He is ashamed. He is as ashamed of it as any right thinking man of God would be ashamed of it, for that reveals Satan for what he is. That is not what Satan wants revealed. He wants to disguise what he is. Satan would seek to hide that sort of devotion because it exposes him.

Of what movements then is Satan proud? Those in which his ministers appear as ministers of light. In one of the major hotels in Dallas, Texas, men posing as ministers of the gospel of Jesus Christ met together to discuss Christian Education. One leader stood up to tell the assembled delegates from all over the United States that the most dangerous thing you can do is to send your child to Sunday school because he will be taught the myths of the Bible, and, when he gets older, he will realize he has to throw out those myths, and he will throw out God along with the myths. Therefore, it is dangerous to send your child to Sunday school.

That man is not a minister of righteousness; he is a minister of the devil. A bishop publicly denied every cardinal doctrine of the Word of God, so much so, that his denomination couldn't tolerate him any longer. He came to one of our Texas universities and told the young people: "Don't let anything or anyone tell you what is sin. You decide for yourself what is sin. And a thing is only sin if you decide it is sin for yourself; and, if you decide it is not sin, then it is not sin." They call that man "Bishop," "shepherd of souls." He is an emissary of the devil, disguised as a minister of light.

Another man, who calls himself the discotheque priest, wanders from cocktail bar to cocktail bar, professing to reach men with the gospel, publicly says, "I don't want to use the word Jesus Christ. I can't understand a god come in the flesh. I want to talk about Jesus because I can understand a man who sweats." Although posing as a minister of light he is speaking as a child of the devil.

Those who know the Word of God and who reverence the authority of the Scriptures need to examine anyone who professes to be a minister of Jesus Christ to see if he can pass this primary test: what is his attitude toward the person and work of Jesus Christ? There is danger in indiscriminate listening to your radio, because Satan who is the prince of the powers of the air can appropriate the airwaves to disseminate his godlessness through those who profess to be ministers of righteousness. The Word of God commands that you try (or test or assay) everyone who professes to be a minister of the Gospel of Christ. Test him according to God's Word, because this is the standard, this is the authority. A man who questions the authority, the integrity, the infallibility and inerrancy of this Book has no guide to his doctrine and has become an emissary of Satan. One who denies the sufficiency of the death of Christ for the salvation of the sinner, regardless of his affiliation or position, is an emissary of Satan, a transformed angel of darkness, who is appearing as an angel of light. One who denies that Jesus Christ is the eternal Son of the eternal God come in the flesh to redeem sinners, no matter how pious his phraseology, no matter what his ecclesiastical endorsement, is an emissary of Satan. Satan is at work to deceive, to perpetrate a lie, and he does it by the subtle imitation of the truth.

Maybe there are some of you who have trusted yourselves in days past to ministers of darkness, thinking they were ministers of light. We call the authority of the Book to witness that there is only one Saviour and that is Jesus Christ; only one plan of salvation, that is that Christ died for our sins; only one way that you can receive God's salvation, and that is to accept Jesus Christ as your personal Saviour. That is the message of light that is in Jesus Christ. We offer such a Saviour to you. Will you trust Him for your salvation?

8

Satan, the Lawless One

II Thessalonians 2:1 - 12

One going to a studio to have his portrait taken will probably suggest to the photographer that he take it from one side or the other because the individual is convinced that one side is better than the other. The photographer may have a different viewpoint and come to a different decision. The individual will select the picture he believes is the most flattering to him.

But no matter from what direction you look at Satan, he has no good side. He is a liar, he is a cheat, he is a deceiver, he is an imitator. We would like to direct your attention to another facet of Satan's character as we see in the Word of God that Satan is portrayed as the lawless one.

The Apostle Paul writing in II Thessalonians 2 reminds us that Satan will consummate his program on the earth during the Tribulation period by introducing to the world one who is called the Man of Sin, the Son of Perdition, or as the phrase might better be translated, the Lawless One. That lawless one who enters so much into the prophetic program is only a manifestation of the basic character of Satan and his program. We will not understand the nature of the warfare in which we are engaged day by day, nor will we understand many of the events unfolding around us in the world today, unless we recognize the fact that the one who is a slanderer, a deceiver, a liar, is also lawless.

Satan was created by an act of God along with the rest of the angelic creation. He came into existence because God spoke. By virtue of the fact that he is a creature, an obligation rested upon him to submit to the authority of the Creator. The Apostle Paul makes it very clear in Romans 9:20, concerning the perplexing doctrine of election, that the created being has no right to say to the Creator, "Why did you make me thus?" For a long time, just how long we do not know, Lucifer abode in the state in which he was placed by creation. As the highest of the created angelic beings, he was an executor of the will of God and an administrator in the realm of angelic beings. As he exercised the power of God, clothed with the glory and brightness as the most beautiful of all created beings, he was superior to all other angels. But as long as there was one who was over him, he was restless. He coveted the authority that belonged to God but, more, he coveted God's independence. When Lucifer saw the independence of God, and he contrasted his obligation to remain in submission to God, within his heart he said, (as is recorded in Isaiah 14:14), "I will be like the most High." And that phase is the epitome of Lucifer's rebellion against God. He never could be like God the Creator, because he was a created being. He never could be like God having eternal life, because he possessed created life. He could be like God in only one way, that is to be responsible to no one other than himself. Thus in his lust for independence, he led a revolt of innumerable host of angels against the authority of God. God comments on the effect of this.

> They that see thee shall narrowly look upon thee, and consider thee, saying, Is this the man that made the earth to tremble, that did shake kingdoms; that made the world as a wilderness and destroyed the cities thereof; that opened not the house of his prisoners? (Isaiah 14:16, 17).

To understand that which Isaiah writes, it is necessary for us to remind ourselves again of the subtlety of Satan's solicitation of Eve to evil. Satan came to her and questioned her knowledge of the revelation of God. He questioned God's love and accused God of being jealous in that He did not want to share His position with anyone; therefore He withheld from Eve that which would be for her good and blessing. And he accused God of imperfection in His character. As a result of this enticement, "when the woman saw that the tree was good for food and that it was pleasant to the eyes, and a tree to be desired to make one wise, she took of the fruit thereof and did eat and gave also unto her husband with her, and he did eat." The first sin of Eve was the sin of doubt, a sin that questioned the character of God. Doubt produced rebellion; and Eve became a rebel against God, the first rebel in this earthly sphere. Adam immediately joined in her rebellion so that there were two rebels. And when Adam and Eve begat children, the children born into their family were born rebels. When they grew this rebelliousness manifested itself as Cain slew his brother, Abel. That was a sin of lawlessness.

Early in the Book of Genesis we find that the whole earth had become so corrupt and so wicked and so rebellious that God saw that the "wickedness of man was great in the earth and that every imagination of the thoughts of his heart was only evil continually. And it repented the Lord that he had made man on the earth, and it grieved him in his heart. And the Lord said, I will destroy man whom I have created from the face of the earth: both man and beast and the creeping things, and the fowl of the air; for it repented me that I have made them" (Genesis 6:5-7).

Now we can begin to understand what Isaiah said when he addressed Satan and asked, "Is this the one that shakes the nations, that causes them to tremble, that turns the earth into a wilderness?" He was speaking of the convulsion of the human race in their espousal of lawlessness and rebellion that caused them to repudiate all law and order, and to rebel against authority. The human race became a rebellious race, rebellious against God. It became a lawless race. God had to send a flood that swept across the face of the earth, to destroy man from the face of it, because Satan had done his work of causing the earth to tremble and to shake and had made the wilderness a desolation in their rebellion against God.

But it was God's purpose to populate the earth again. He used Noah and his wife, and their children, a small family who had been brought to faith in God because God had revealed Himself to them. The earth was repopulated after the flood, and to prevent the shaking of the earth by lawlessness, we find in the ninth chapter of Genesis that God instituted human government. And human government was given power up to and including death over the individual so that lawlessness should be curbed and that men might have justice and righteousness on the earth. The principle laid down in Genesis 9:6 is: "Whoso sheddeth man's blood, by man shall his blood be shed, for in the image of God made he man."

The Apostle Paul comments on the prerogatives and the purpose of government in the epistle to the Romans, chapter thirteen. Paul commands: "Let every soul be subject unto the higher powers. For there is no power but of God: the powers that be are ordained of God. Whosoever therefore resisteth the power, resisteth the ordinance of God: and they that resist shall receive to themselves damnation. For rulers are not a terror to good works but to the evil. Wilt thou, then, not be afraid of the power? do that which is good and thou shalt have praise of the same: for he is the minister of God to thee for good. But if thou do that which is evil, be afraid; for he [that is the governor], beareth not the sword in vain: for he is the minister of God, a revenger to execute wrath upon him that doeth evil." In this passage, the Apostle very, very clearly tells us that rulers and authorities in the civil realm are appointed by God; they are called by God his ministers. They are not ministers of the Gospel, but they are administrators of law and order, of right and justice. They are raised up to administer God's judgment upon evil doers, to punish the evildoers and to preserve those that do well. Lest you think this is an isolated passage notice, in I Peter 2:13, where the Apostle says we are to submit ourselves " . . . to every ordinance of man for the Lord's sake: whether it be to the king as supreme; or unto governors, as unto them that are sent by him for the punishment of evildoers, and for the praise of them that do well."

In Titus we have the same teaching given to us by the Apostle Paul once again. Paul was concerned that these who had been brought to freedom in Jesus Christ should recognize that they were under the authority of government and were to submit to it because government was a divine institution necessitated by the rebellion of Satan and by Satan's program to produce utter lawlessness upon the face of the earth. We remind you that the

Apostle Paul was living under one of the most corrupt, one of the most authoritarian governments that the world had ever seen. Yet Paul never took it upon himself to criticize the form of the government but said that believers had a responsibility to submit to that government.

This leads us to the conclusion that any form of government that fulfills the divine purpose for government, that is, any government that maintains law and order, that curbs lawlessness and prevents riot, is a government that has divine approval. And the believer is responsible to submit to it. We are trying to impress upon you that God had a purpose for human government. Human government was necessitated because Satan is lawless, is a rebel, and it is his purpose to turn men to lawlessness, to rebellion against society, against God, against God's law. And to prevent the work of the one who causes the nations to tremble, God has instituted human government.

Satan has quite a different purpose. We saw it in Genesis chapter six concerning the flood. Satan's purpose is to turn the whole world into a lawless chaos. It is his purpose to cause men and nations to rebel against the rule of God, against the moral standards of the Word of God and the character of God so that lawlessness results. We have a passage in which Paul describes the character of society in the last days when Satan's work is unrestrained. II Timothy 3:1-5 in the Amplified translation reads:

> But understand this, that in the last days there will set in perilous times of great stress *and* trouble — hard to deal with and hard to bear. For people will be lovers of self *and* [utterly] self-centered, lovers of money *and* aroused by an inordinate (greedy) desire for wealth, proud *and* arrogant *and* contemptuous boasters. They will be abusive (blasphemous, scoffers), disobedient to parents, ungrateful, unholy and profane. [They will be] without natural (human) affection (callous and inhuman), relentless — admitting of no truce *or* appeasement. [They will be] slanderers — false accusers, trouble makers; intemperate *and* loose in morals and conduct, uncontrolled *and* fierce, haters of good. [They will be] treacherous (betrayers), rash [and] inflated with selfconceit. [They will be] lovers of sensual pleasures *and* vain amusements more than *and* rather than lovers of God. For [although] they hold a form of piety (true religion),

they deny *and* reject *and* are strangers to the power of it — their conduct belies the genuineness of their profession. Avoid [all] such people — turn away from them.

Such is the picture of lawlessness as Satan seeks to promote it in the earth in these last days.

The believer is confronted with this work of Satan in the world around him. He also experiences the work of Satan in his own heart, for Satan can produce lawlessness in society as a whole only by producing lawlessness in individuals in that society. And so Satan's method is to cause the nation to stumble, to catapult society into lawlessness and rebellion against authority by leading individuals into that same state of lawlessness and riot.

When an individual is born into this world, he is born with a lawless, rebellious nature. That was your nature and mine before we were saved. When we were saved, God brought us under authority to Himself and put us under control of Jesus Christ. But we still retain all of the old rebelliousness against the rule of God and against the holiness and righteousness of God that we had before we were saved. And unless the Spirit of God brings us into subjection, rebelliousness will manifest itself later.

We little realize the extent of the unrestrained lawlessness that is abroad in the world today and more specifically that is abroad in our own nation today. This development of lawlessness is an indication that we are in the endtimes before the appearing of the Lord of Glory who will bring this earth into subjection to Himself. It is also a danger signal for our nation.

No nation in the history of the world has ever been founded without a regard for law and order at its inception. And no nation has been destroyed until that regard for law and order was first destroyed. Think of Babylon, the great nation that overshadowed all the other nations in Old Testament history. Out of Babylon came some of the greatest codified law that became a standard for all other nations. But as you turn to the prophecy of Daniel on the eve of Babylon's destruction, what do you find? You find the king in a great banqueting hall riotously drinking and repudiating all gods. That nation that had been founded on law disregarded law, and in one night it was swept away and its power broken. What was the greatness of Rome? It was the *Lex Romana,* Roman Law. The legal system that Rome developed became the foundation of the Roman Empire. But read Gibbons *Rise and Fall of the Roman Empire* and what do you find? At the period of Rome's decline citizens had repudiated law and its right to rule over them, and nationally and individually, they did as they pleased. They were swept away by invaders from the North. When they repudiated law they went into decline and decay.

Our nation was founded upon the Word of God, upon respect for the authority of God, upon respect for a legitimate government. We recently have entered into a period when lawlessness has become the accepted practice of the day. When marches designed to defy the law of the land are organized to show open rebellion, it is an indication of how far along the path of lawlessness we as a nation have gone. And councils of churches and so-called Christian organizations join in with this godless, Satanic movement, and seek to overthrow the law of the land and the rule by law. Churches have contributed to the Satanic program seeking to destroy that which is the primary function of government. This is far more than individual rebellion. It is organized lawlessness against the authority of state. Civil disobedience as an instrument to change governments or compel governments to do the will of the people is a part of a Satanic system that seeks to disregard law. Lawlessness does not become legitimate because it is organized.

When those in high office say that it is ridiculous to expect a man to obey a law that he does not like, they are advocating lawlessness. And when one whose office it is to uphold law and order advocates rebellion because the law does not suit him, he is promoting Satan's great purpose in the world today, to destroy nations by producing lawlessness. It is to be questioned whether Rome ever went any further in lawlessness than we have already gone. And for Rome there could be nothing but dissolution. It is to be questioned whether we have gone any further in our godlessness than Babylon had gone. We are where Belshazzar was when he "drank wine and praised the gods of gold . . ."

(Daniel 5:4). God judged and overthrew that nation! This same lawlessness has pervaded the warp and woof of the fabric of our society. And that is what Isaiah meant when he said Satan would shake the nations by producing national disregard for law.

Now in order to keep the individual from falling onto this purpose of Satan, God has placed authority in several realms. The believer is charged to be in submission to that authority. The area of government, to which the believer is to be in subjection, is only one area of authority that we are called upon to respect. There is authority in the home. And God by divine appointment has constituted the husband as the head of the home. Those in the home are to recognize that the authority of the husband and the father is a God-given authority. Authority was given to the husband and the father to curb lawlessness. The husband, himself lawless, must be in absolute subjection to Christ. Children are naturally lawless; they are to be in submission to their parents. And the wife is to be in subjection to her husband to curb lawlessness. Satan will seek to produce rebellion in the home. This might be prevented through the exercise of authority.

The Word tells us that God has constituted authority in the church. That authority has been placed in elders, and the believers in the assembly are commanded to be in subjection to the elders (I Peter 5:5). Why? Because believers can be just as rebellious and lawless as anyone else. And God, who has given authority in the state, and who has given authority in the home, has also set up authority in the church. You will notice these are the three spheres in which a man lives; the sphere of society or the state, the sphere of church, and the sphere of home. There is no area in which we live in which God has not provided authority, authority which was necessary because our adversary is a lawless one, and we are lawless by nature. And lest Satan get an advantage over us and bring us into subjection to himself, God has imposed this authority upon us.

There is yet another authority, the authority that belongs to one whose name is to be King of kings, and Lord of lords. God has given Jesus Christ not only to be Saviour but God has given Him to be our Lord. And when you use the term *Lord* in connection with Jesus Christ, you are confessing that God has given Him to you to be your authority, the One who will rule over you, who will control you. For what purpose? To prevent the lawlessness of Satan from being reproduced in you. The believer who is in subjection to Jesus Christ will be in subjection in the state, in the home, and in the church. But God's method of assuring subjection in each of these areas is to bring us into subjection, first of all, to Jesus Christ.

The child who is in subjection to Jesus Christ will be in subjection to parents, because the parent is the channel through whom Christ operates. The child of God who is in subjection to Christ will be in subjection to the state because he recognizes the state is a channel through which Christ exercises His authority. The child of God who is in subjection to the Lord Jesus Christ will be in subjection to the elders because he recognizes the elders are one channel through which Christ operates.

The child of God must make a decision concerning whose authority he will recognize over him. Satan bids for that authority. Over against that Jesus Christ stretches forth a nail-pierced hand and invites you to take His yoke upon you. He invites you to take up your cross and follow Him as the Lord who has the right to rule over you. You have no power to combat the lawlessness of Satan and, your voice raised against the lawlessness of the land will be a tiny voice. But you can prevent Satan from ruling over you individually. You can prevent it only by turning your life over completely to Jesus Christ so that He might exercise His sovereign authority over you as the Lord over his servant. The deceiver will blind you to the truth, the liar will deny the truth, the lawless rebel will seek to cause you to revolt against the truth. Only as you put yourself in the hand of the Lord Jesus Christ can you be delivered from this evil one.

9

Satan, the Rebel

Job 1:13 - 22

Since God is the Creator, all glory, honor and majesty, all power, dominion and authority belong to Him. The primary responsibility resting upon the creature is to be in subjection to the Creator. Lucifer, the wisest and the most beautiful of all God's created beings, rebelled against that responsibility. His desire was to depose God from His throne and displace God as the supreme authority in the universe which God had created. In his rebellion Lucifer led a vast number of created angelic beings after him and they like him became rebels.

When God created Adam and placed him in the garden of Eden, He placed one requirement on him: to submit to Him and to obey Him. And so that there should be an opportunity to demonstrate this submission to the authority of God, God placed the tree of the knowledge of good and evil in the garden and said to Adam, "Thou shalt not eat of it: for in the day that thou eatest thereof thou shalt surely die" (Genesis 2:17). Satan, the rebel, had one burning, consuming passion within himself, to lead Adam and Eve in his path of rebellion against God. His temptation in the Garden was the temptation to rebel. Adam followed Eve's rebellion, and the entire race that sprang from these two was a lawless, rebellious one.

The plan of Satan to lead men in rebellion is perhaps no more clearly illustrated than in the encounter between God, Satan and Job as it is recorded in the first two chapters of the book of Job. From the record there we discover that Satan's purpose for Job was identical with his purpose for Adam. His purpose for you is the same. Satan's great desire is to lead you to rebel against God. Satan is as much concerned about your rebellion against God as any other one thing. He is not so concerned about getting you enmeshed in some heinous sin as he is in causing you to rebel against God, since that is the start of every sin. This is clearly brought out in the experience of Job.

Job had been blessed materially as perhaps no man of his generation had been blessed. The Scripture records God's blessing upon him in his family, for he had seven sons and three daughters. In addition, God had multiplied his material wealth in that he had seven thousand sheep and three thousand camels, five hundred yoke of oxen and five hundred she asses and a very great household (that is of servants or slaves to take care of the flocks and herds and to provide for the family). All of this was recognized as a blessing from God. Job took no credit for it as though by his own wisdom, might or power he had accumulated it. In receiving this wealth, he responded by worshiping God. He recognized that God who had given could just as quickly take it all away. It was testified of Job in the first verse that he was a man who was perfect and upright, one that feared God and eschewed (or hated or was afraid of being enmeshed in) evil. The evidence that Job was perfect and upright was that he feared God. His perfection was not only evident to his family and his acquaintances, but also to God, for Job showed his perfection and uprightness by abiding in the rightful relationship of a creature to the Creator. He feared, he respected, he submitted to, he bowed to the authority of God who had given these blessings to him.

Job's life was characterized by constant worship. He did not come on some stated occasion to a thanksgiving service to look back over the past year to enumerate God's blessings. Thanksgiving was his daily attitude, for in the fifth verse of the first chapter we are told, ". . . when the days of their feasting were gone about, that Job sent and sanctified them, and rose up early in the morning, and offered burnt-offerings according to the number of them all: for Job said, It may be that my sons have sinned, and cursed God in their hearts. Thus did Job continually." Job was a priest in the family and daily he offered sacrifices to

God. He reaffirmed by that sacrifice his continuing dependence upon and submission to God. As the priest he was declaring that his sons who were under his authority were also subject to the authority of God.

The thing that Job feared more than anything else was that his sons would be rebels, for he said, "perhaps it may be that my sons have sinned and cursed God in their hearts." How would Job suspect the possibility that his sons might curse God? After all, they had been brought up in his family and he had trained them and taught them and set an example of submission and dependence upon God. But Job still feared that his sons might turn out to be rebels. Job knew what was in his own heart. He obviously had felt the enticements of Satan to some act of rebellion himself. Since he, the head of the home, the spiritual as well as the physical father, felt these temptations, he knew that his sons would be subject to those temptations. Therefore he guarded against that rebellion by continued sacrifice to God lest he or his family should curse God in their hearts. Thus God has shown what kind of a man Job was, a man who exercised conscious dependence upon God.

Satan could not rest as long as there was a creature who willfully and voluntarily submitted himself to the authority of God instead of giving himself to do the will of Satan. It seems that Satan's whole attention was focused upon this one man to the exclusion of all the other members of his generation. Satan wasn't concerned with some of Job's friends who were already rebels. It was Job whom Satan desired to lead in rebellion and to bring into subjection to himself because of Job's dependence upon God.

May we point out to you that when any child of God by the Holy Spirit makes it his purpose to live a life so as to please the Lord Jesus Christ and to walk in complete dependence upon God, he is exposing himself to all the fiery darts of the wicked one. Don't think because you voluntarily submit your will to the will of God that that submission is going to be the end of struggling with temptation. Unfortunately, that is the beginning of it. As long as you walk in a path of rebellion against God, Satan will leave you alone. The Spirit of God won't, but Satan will! When you set it as your purpose to walk so as to please the One who called you unto holiness, Satan will make you his special target. That is what he did with Job.

When the occasion came that Satan was given audience before the throne of God, it was Job whom God singled out as an object lesson to Satan. God took great pleasure in pointing to Job as a man in whose worship He found delight, one in whose submission He found satisfaction. Satan accused God of having bought Job. He said, "Doth Job fear God for nought?" (Job 1:9). If God is not worshiped because He is worthy to be worshiped, then the worship means nothing to God. God is not honored and glorified until His creatures worship Him voluntarily. That is why worship is always viewed in the Word of God as a voluntary sacrifice. Some sacrifices were required. There were also voluntary sacrifices. God was satisfied through the obedience that brought the required sacrifices. But God was worshiped through the voluntary sacrifices that men brought because they loved Him, because they respected Him, because they recognized His right to worship.

So Satan stood in front of God and insulted Him. He said to God, in effect, "You bought Job with your blessings; You bought his worship; You bought his obedience; he would be insane not to continue this ritual so that You would continue Your material blessings to him." This was Satan's challenge: "Put forth thy hand now and touch all that he has and he will curse thee to thy face" (Job 1:11). What did Satan want Job to do more than anything else? Curse God. Rebel against God. Satan's concept was that God was not worthy of worship apart from His gifts. This cursing did not require an oath from his lips. If Job had lifted his eyes to heaven and had asked, "Why?" it would have been rebellion. He would have followed Satan's plan. God would have been dishonored through what would seem to be an innocent question. The messengers came to Job. The first in verse 14 said that all of his oxen and asses were either driven off or slain. The second in verse 16 reported all of his flocks and herds and sheep were destroyed. The third in verse 17 told that all of his camels had fallen into the hands of the Chaldeans. The fourth, in verses 18 and 19, relayed the news that his ten children were lost in a storm. Within a few moments everything that Job had was taken away; Job was a pauper, bereft of his children and his possessions.

His faith, even in this testing, was unshakable. Even though possibly he was tempted to do what Satan wanted him to do, "to curse God," it is recorded in verse 20 that, "Job arose, and rent his mantle, and shaved his head." These were signs of mourning. Job was not oblivious to the facts. Job did not deny that this tragedy had taken place. He did not move into a world where he was withdrawn from reality. The rending of his garment shows that he was fully conscious of the import of what these messengers had brought to him. But instead of cursing God he "fell down upon the ground, and worshiped." Job was as much a worshiper when everything had been taken away as he was when unmeasured bounty was bestowed upon him by God. This is one of the worst defeats that Satan had ever suffered. Few, if any, had been subjected to the testing to which Job was subjected by Satan to get him to renounce God. Job was sustained by his recognition of dependence upon God, upon the goodness of the character of God, upon the trustworthiness of God's wisdom. Satan had expected to hear curses of wrath pour forth from the lips of Job. However, he was humiliated and chagrined to hear words of praise flow from the lips of this saint of God.

When a man comes into testing it is too late to learn to worship. It is too late to learn to trust. It is too late to learn to walk by faith. A man can be triumphant through a testing of Satan by walking with God daily before the storms and the trials and tests come. Job was able to worship in the time of trial because worship had become the established pattern of his life. His dependence of former days continued even during this onslaught of Satan.

Although Satan had suffered a most humiliating defeat, he was ready to challenge God again. God once again pointed his finger to Job, the one individual on the face of the earth whom Satan most wanted to forget. He asked the question again, "Have you considered my servant Job?" (Job 2:3). To paraphrase that question, God is asking, "Satan, how do you explain a man like Job?" The only rightful answer could be, "Job acknowledges depend-

ence upon You because of what You are, and worships." But
Satan had another explanation and he challenged God a second
time, ". . . skin for skin, yea, all that a man hath will he give
for his life. But put forth thine hand now, and touch his bone
and his flesh, and he will curse thee to thy face" (Job 2:4, 5).
What one thing did Satan want to produce in Job? Rebellion!
Satan suggests that since Job submitted to the Creator, as Creator
He should touch the lips He had created, and when He did, Job
would renounce His right to rule, and rebel.

Once again with God's permission Satan went forth from the
presence of the Lord with the avowed purpose of working to
make Job repeat the sin of rebellion, his own first sin, the sin of
the angels, and the sin of Adam and Eve. And we find in the 8th
verse, ". . . and he sat down among the ashes." The ash heap
was outside the city. It was an unclean place. It was where the
outcasts went. Job had cut himself off from his home now. He
had cut himself off from his wife, the only one left to him. Cutting himself off from all of his friends, he felt that he had been
abandoned. It is then the temptation came. Notice the subtlety
of Satan here. Satan did not approach directly but he approached
Job through his wife, and his wife became the agent of temptation. Eve was tested as Satan approached her in the form of a
creature. Job was subjected to a greater test than Eve because
this solicitation came from the one who was nearest and dearest
to him. The strategy of Satan is not to use someone who would
be easy to repel but to use the one whom it is most difficult to
deny. But the temptation is unchanged because Satan's purpose
is unchanged. Job's wife came to him and said, "Dost thou still
retain thine integrity? [thy dependence upon God] curse God,
and die." In mouthing those words she is promoting the purpose
of Satan and is putting a satanic temptation before him to do
the one thing that Satan wants Job to do more than anything
else in this world, to abandon his dependence, his submission,
his obedience; to become independent of God.

How God gloried in Job's response (verse 10). He reproved
his wife, and said, "You speak as one of the foolish women
speaketh." *Foolish* in the Word of God has to do with one who

has left God out of his thinking. He said, "You are talking like a godless one when you invite me to do what Satan wants the human race to do." "Shall we receive good at the hand of God, and shall we not receive evil? In all this did not Job sin with his lips" (Job 2:10). Job refused to declare himself independent of God because of his faith in the character of God and his recognition of his responsibility to submit to God.

What Satan wanted for Job summarizes what Satan wants for you and me. It is not his desire that you should go rob a bank, that you should embezzle a large sum from your employer, that you should be involved in some great ethical or moral scandal. That is not his plan for you at all. What he wants is for you to rebel against God. Say "no" to Him; deny Him His right to exercise absolute authority over you. When you do that you have fallen into the sin of Eve; you have robbed God of His glory, His right to be obeyed and worshiped.

Job was not the only one subjected to such a test. In the 16th chapter of the gospel of Matthew we see our Lord walking with His disciples. He turned to them with a question and said, verse 13, "Whom do men say that I the Son of man am?" The disciples began to repeat the answers that they had heard. Some explained the person of Christ as John the Baptist: some, Elias (Elijah); some Jeremiah; some, one of the prophets. Then after reporting what they had overheard, our Lord turned to the disciples directly and said, "Whom say ye that I am?" Peter as the spokesman for the twelve confessed his faith, "Thou art the Christ (Messiah), the Son of the living God." Christ followed that affirmation of faith with a further revelation. He told them, in the 21st verse, "that He must go unto Jerusalem, and suffer many things of the elders and chief priests and scribes, and be killed, and be raised again the third day." That was all part of the prophecy as to what Messiah would do. Isaiah 53 had said that the Messiah, whom Peter has just confessed the Lord to be, was to be the suffering servant who would give Himself as a sacrifice for sins that through the shedding of His blood He might provide salvation for sinners. When our Lord, upon Peter's confession, said, "Yes, I am Messiah and I even now am on My way to Jerusalem to give Myself as a sacrifice for the sins of the world," Peter reached out and put his hand on the shoulders of the Lord Jesus and began to shake Him, so as to shake some sense into Him. So he said, "Lord be it far from thee: this shall not be unto Thee." Now notice our Lord's reply, "Get thee behind Me, Satan."

Just as Satan used Mrs. Job as the channel to put temptation before Job to renounce God's will for Job, so Satan used the disciple who was as close to Christ as any of the disciples to put his temptation before Christ. What was it? To rebel against the will of God because God had set Christ apart to a cross. Turn from the way of God, leave Jerusalem, flee to safety in Galilee. Jesus Christ recognized that word for what it was, a temptation from Satan, and He addressed Peter, not as the originator of that statement but as Satan, the one who had given Peter that thought. He said, "Get thee behind Me, Satan. Thou art an offence to Me: for thou savourest not the things that be of God, but those that be of men." Satan had no greater purpose for the Lord Jesus Christ than to divert His feet from the path of perfect obedience to the will of God. He put that temptation before Christ through the lips of Peter.

It was only a little while later that our Lord came into the garden of Gethsemane. The tempter was even there. Christ resisted that same temptation to abandon the will of God for Him when He bowed before the Father and said, "Not My will but Thine be done." He was obedient unto death. That is why the writer to the book of Hebrews invites us to look unto Jesus "the author and finisher of our faith; who for the joy that was set before Him endured the cross, despising the shame . . . " (Hebrews 12:2). The joy set before Christ was the joy of being perfectly obedient and submissive to the will of God.

That which was Satan's avowed purpose for Job and that which was Satan's purpose for Christ — to turn them from submission and dependence and obedience to God — is Satan's chief desire for you day-by-day and step-by-step. Be on guard against rebellion. God asks you to continue in the place of obedience, the place of subjection, the place of a worshiper as you recognize God's right to your life.

10

Pursued by a Roaring Lion

I Peter 5:1 - 11

The Apostle Peter, as a faithful shepherd, was preparing his sheep for the kind of life that they would have to live from day to day. It was a difficult life, for the Gospel was not acceptable in the society in which they moved. Religiously, men were self-satisfied and looked down on this which threatened to overthrow the old established religions in which they had been brought up. Politically, Christianity was not acceptable because it looked forward to the coming of the Lord Jesus Christ who as King of kings and Lord of lords would set up a kingdom and would subject all nations to His own authority. Economically, those who were in the Christian church were suffering privation and hunger because they had left the established system.

The Apostle Peter, in view of these problems, wrote his first Epistle to enable these scattered, suffering believers to survive their persecution. Having dealt first with what seemed to be the most extreme forms of persecution, he speaks of the greatest persecution from the greatest persecutor, that is from Satan himself. He concludes this little epistle as a faithful shepherd, "Be sober, be vigilant because your adversary the devil, as a roaring lion, walketh about seeking whom he may devour" (I Peter 5:8). The admonition that Peter gives is in four words; Be sober, be vigilant.

Sobriety, in Scripture, has little, if anything, to do with the use of alcoholic beverages. Sobriety has to do with a serious attitude of the mind. It has to do with an outlook on life. Sobriety sees things in their true light. One who is serious-minded sees things in their true nature, because he has a scriptural set of values and

93

is living in the light of those new principles that have been given to him by Jesus Christ. An individual who takes no cognizance of the nature or character of the world, one who is unmindful of the purposes and the attacks of our adversary, the Devil, can afford to live in a lighthearted or flippant way. But for one who sees life as Jesus Christ sees it, there must be an entirely new attitude, an entirely new outlook characterized by sobriety.

But in addition to this serious-minded attitude, the believer is to be vigilant. Vigilant means to watch carefully, to look around. One becomes vigilant when he recognizes the presence of an enemy or an adversary. Whereas sobriety deals with his internal attitude, vigilance deals with the external defense. This new attitude within is necessary because of the attack from without. So the child of God must recognize that he is living in the midst of an hostile enemy, that he is surrounded by an unseen adversary seeking to destroy him. He knows he must make his way through a morass where there is ample opportunity for the adversary to hide, where there is abundant opportunity for ambush. It is inconceivable that our men in Vietnam could make a foray into enemy territory without exercising vigilance and serious-mindedness. Having seen a buddy destroyed by the adversary's bullets would produce a serious-mindedness. The consciousness that behind every bush might lurk an enemy who already has one in his gunsight would produce vigilance. A man would be an utter idiot to go into armed combat with any other attitude or outlook. And yet how many of us as God's children treat life as though it were a Sunday school picnic at which we make our way to the table to get a drink of pink lemonade!

Peter, after commanding us to be sober and vigilant, tells us why this is necessary. "Your adversary, the devil, as a roaring lion walketh about seeking whom he may devour." When Peter uses the pronoun *your*, he is addressing believers. Satan is not the adversary of those who are already in his family. He is the adversary of those who have been born *out* of any relationship to him by faith in Jesus Christ. He is speaking of those who once were subject to Satan as their father, their dictator, their lord, their god. Now, having come to know the Lord Jesus Christ, they have recognized that Christ has a greater authority, that His right to be obeyed supercedes the demands of Satan. They have recognized the lie of Satan for what it is and they have received the truth that is in Jesus Christ. Because they have repudiated him and by faith have received Jesus Christ as Saviour and Lord, they have incensed and antagonized Satan.

Satan does not release his subjects willingly or easily. The very fact that one is snatched as a brand out of the burning and becomes a child of God unleashes all of the wrath of hell against him because he is now an insult to Satan. Because you have received Jesus Christ you have antagonized Satan and made an adversary out of him. There is no neutrality in Satan's attitude toward you, and you would be satanically deceived if you think that Satan does not care what you do now that you are no longer his. You personally are willing to let someone else's children alone, for you have enough problems with your own. That is not the attitude of Satan. He lets his own alone and traffics with God's children. As soon as you become the child of God then Satan becomes your adversary.

Satan is not omnipresent. God is omnipresent, and God the Father, Son, and Holy Spirit can give personal attention to you as though you were the only creature existing on the face of the earth. The infinite love, attention, interest, care, and provision of God is directed to you. But Satan is not omnipresent. How then can he give you so much trouble? Satan is an organizer and he has things well-organized in his kingdom. He had a good pattern to follow. Even though God is omnipotent, omnipresent and omniscient, God administers the affairs of His kingdom through created beings, angels. God sovereignly assigns to each one who shall be an heir of salvation a guardian angel. It works well, for God's angels in perfect obedience fulfill the will of God, so that none whom God has chosen to salvation are ever lost.

When Lucifer rebelled against God he took with him an innumerable host of angels who gave to him the authority that rightly belonged to God. They acknowledged him as god and submitted to him. Satan imitates God's plan of administration, and carries out his diabolical plans through these fallen angels, the demons. Although Satan cannot be personally present with you, yet through his demons, he can exercise authority over you, and he can order the demons in subjection to him to do what he wants to accomplish in your life. Satan will not let his demons relax their attack against you day or night. In unseen but constant warfare, the adversary openly attacks the believer to divert him from the path of obedience to the Word of God.

This attack of Satan is emphasized when the Apostle says, "Your adversary walketh about." This word is in the present tense and you wouldn't be amiss in reading, "Your adversary, the Devil, constantly walks about, or constantly stalks." Satan never relaxes. You sleep. He doesn't; he is planning for the next day's attack. You sit in church. So does Satan. He doesn't leave you alone. He doesn't stay outside; he is there to attack and to divert and to snatch away the Word that is being sown.

The Apostle uses a graphic picture to try to convey to us Satan's ceaseless and destructive activity, the figure of a lion. The lion, who stalks the prey driven by hunger, is not stalking it to admire the beautiful coat, the grace with which the animal moves; the lion stalks because it is bent upon the destruction of that which it has chosen as its prey. Satan is pictured here as a roaring lion that stalks. "Roaring" lion suggests that Satan considers he has already conquered his prey. No lion stalking its prey announces the fact by roaring. The lion does not emerge from sleep, go out into the plain driven by hunger where animals are grazing and announce to them that he is on the prowl. It moves with swiftness and silence; it strikes and destroys the prey and then roars. That roar does two things. First of all it is a note of triumph in which the lion trumpets out his conquest. Because the lion is cowardly, it is also a warning to any other animals to stay away while he enjoys the fruits of the kill.

It is important for us to relate these things to Satan. We think that Satan will roar like a gentleman to announce that he is in the area and that, after he tells us what he is up to, then we can look for cover. We have been deceived into thinking we can take time to get on our armament and prepare to meet him. How Satan has deceived us about his method of operation! Satan is

not going to reveal his presence to you until he can roar in triumph. When Satan roars he is not roaring to announce to you
that he has destroyed you. You already know that. After he has
destroyed or overthrown the child of God, he roars in defiance
against Almighty God, to challenge Him to do something about
the devastation that he has wrought. When Lucifer first rebelled
he said, "I will exalt my throne above the stars of God. I will be
like the most High." When Satan leads some of God's children
into sin he roars to defy God because he thinks that he has
brought himself one step closer to his goal to remove God from
His throne and to rule over God's universe.

Scripture gives a number of illustrations of how Satan as a
roaring lion does go about seeking whom he may devour. Look
first of all into II Samuel 11, the record of David's sin. Notice
how Satan operated here to observe the principle, how he stealthily, quietly, destroyed. Verse 1 tells us that this incident took
place at the time when kings went forth to battle. God had given
David singular victories in battle. Under David's reign the
boundaries of Israel were extended to their widest sphere in
history. These were God's victories, and this obviously was a time
of God's blessing on David. Because David sensed God's blessing
and was conscious of God's presence with him, he did not watch
with sobriety. In the second verse we are told, "And it came to
pass at evening time that David arose from off his bed, and
walked upon the roof of the king's house." It would seem to
suggest that David had retired for the night. He had received
reports of the victories in battle. He had gone to bed satisfied
that God's hand was still upon him in blessing. For some reason
or another David was sleepless. Perhaps it was because of the
heat, for when David arose he went to the housetop. If any
breeze were stirring at all it would be up there. He went alone
to be cooled by the breeze. It seemed such a natural thing to do,
a time when a man could relax. He was not anticipating sin. But
as he walked on the roof he saw a beautiful woman washing herself. He sent for her and fell into sin. Did David plan this?
No. Did he anticipate it? No. Was there something that David
had done wrong that led up to this? No. But Satan was there

as an adversary stealthily stalking the child of God, and David fell before the temptation and committed a sin that brought reproach upon himself and upon his God. When David least expected it, an opportunity was afforded Satan to pounce, and he did so because David was not sober and watchful.

Consider another incident. In Luke 22:31, our Lord said, "Simon, Simon, behold, Satan hath desired to have you, that he may sift you as wheat: But I have prayed for thee, that thy faith fail not. . . . " These words follow almost immediately upon one of the most precious experiences that the disciples had had with their Lord. Christ had had the disciples prepare the Passover, that memorial that looked back to deliverance out of Egypt and looked ahead to the remission of sins as it would be provided by the Messiah who would give Himself as the sacrificial Lamb. After the Passover supper, as we read in John chapters 14, 15 and 16, our Lord had bared His heart and shared His feelings with the disciples. He had instructed them of the new intimacy into which they would be brought with Him following His death and resurrection. Our Lord had reached out and had drawn these men intimately into His own heart. They were occupied with Him. His words filled their minds and His love filled their hearts. Yet, our Lord said, "Peter, Satan is right here and he desires to sift you as wheat." Our Lord made His way out to the garden; thrice He bowed before the Father and prayed, "Not my will, but thine be done." But His time of intimacy with the Father was terminated by the band of soldiers who took Christ before the presence of the High Priest. Everyone's attention was focused upon these two figures, the High Priest in his beautiful garments, and the Lord Jesus Christ who stood there to be tried by the priest. Everyone was listening to the dialog between Christ and the priest.

Who was paying any attention to Peter out there in the dark alongside the fire? Satan was not paying the least bit of attention to what the priest was saying or what Christ was saying. Satan's attention was focused upon Peter. We read in Luke 22:54, "Peter followed afar off. And when they had kindled a fire in the midst of the hall, and were set down together, Peter sat down among them. But a certain maid beheld him as he sat by the fire, and earnestly looked upon him, and said, This man was also with him. And he denied him, saying, Woman, I know him not." Almost immediately after the time of Peter's richest blessing with Christ in the Upper Room comes this denial. Why? Because Peter was not sober and vigilant. Satan was looking for opportunity, and, finding that opportunity, he pounced.

We find the principle again in Acts chapter 5. In Acts 4:32-37 a band of believers who had been excommunicated from the temple met together. They put all their possessions into a common treasury, and each man's needs were met out of that treasury. They were enjoying an intimacy of fellowship, for they were driven together for mutual support because of the persecution from the unbelieving religious and political world. It would seem that if ever there were a group that would be sober and vigilant it would be that little group. Yet we read that Ananias sold a possession and "kept back part of the price, his wife also being privy to it, and brought a certain part, and laid it at the apostles' feet. But Peter said, Ananias, why hath Satan filled thine heart to lie to the Holy Ghost, and to keep back part of the price of the land?" Judgment fell upon Ananias and a little while later upon his wife, Sapphira. Why? Because Satan had been watching for an opportunity, and when he found it he pounced and then roared his defiance in the face of God.

Sin is not necessarily the result of a premeditated plan. Sin often comes to a believer because the believer was not serious minded, recognizing the nature of the conflict, and vigilant. He gave Satan an opportunity and Satan took the opportunity and used it to defeat the child of God in his Christian life.

The Apostle recognizes this danger in Ephesians 4:27 when he gives the command, "Neither give place to the devil." In II Corinthians 2:10, 11 Paul says, "To whom ye forgive any thing, I forgive also: for if I forgave anything, to whom I forgave it, for your sakes forgave I it in the person of Christ; Lest *Satan should get an advantage of us. . . .*" The word *advantage* means a toe hold. One scaling a mountain does not need a road to get to the top. A skilled mountain climber can make his way on the ice fields and up sheer granite walls if he can get or make as much as a toe hold. He doesn't take a bulldozer and bulldoze a road to the top. Give him a toehold and he can ascend the highest mountain. We somehow have felt that unless we provide Satan a four-lane paved super-highway he can't attack us or overcome us or defeat us. Peter didn't believe that; nor did Paul. Paul was afraid that Satan would get an advantage by getting a toe hold. In a military maneuver all that is needed is a beachhead. From that beachhead the army can launch a successful attack.

Satan is looking for a beachhead and if he can establish a toehold or a beachhead in your life, he can destroy you. Satan can establish a beachhead by causing you to doubt. If you begin to doubt the authority of the Word of God, you have given Satan a beachhead upon which he can launch a campaign that will overthrow your faith. You don't have to throw the Bible away; just harbor a single doubt about the truth that is revealed in the book and you have given Satan a beachhead to destroy your faith. He doesn't have to get you to deny the holiness and the righteousness of God to pervert your conduct. All he has to do is get you to turn the least bit from the path of perfect obedience to God and he, from that beachhead, can destroy a life.

The apostles recognized this danger; they recognized there is never a moment, day or night, day in and day out, when your footsteps are not being pursued by an adversary who is watching every move that you make. The first time you provide him with a beachhead he will establish himself on that beachhead and he will begin his work from it. But he cannot do it unless you provide him the opportunity. He cannot overpower the defenses of the Holy Spirit nor can Satan penetrate the armor that has been provided through the Word of God as the Apostle outlines it in Ephesians. You must give him the beachhead; you must give him the opportunity.

Peter was concerned that those who are facing persecution from the world, from the government, from the established religion of the day, should realize that those were not their real danger, nor were those systems the real adversary. The real adversary was Satan who dogged every step, who pursued them every moment of every day without fail, and who was watching for the smallest opportunity in order that he might seize it. David gave him an opportunity by taking a second look. Peter provided him a toehold by being afraid. Ananias gave him a beachhead by harboring greed and fostering a lie. Those who provided him the opportunity found out that he was ready to occupy the territory.

If you would stand against your adversary, you must be serious minded, that is recognizing the nature of the conflict in which you are engaged. You must be watchful, recognizing that Satan is dogging your steps every moment you live. You must maintain an unbroken dependence upon the Spirit of God. You must use the armor that God has provided that you might be able to stand against the fiery darts of the wicked one. Therefore, because of the nature of our adversary, be sober, be vigilant.

11

The Doctrine of Satan

II Peter 1:16 – 2:2

If you were looking for Satan and knew only that he was disguised, where would you go to look for him? The corner bar? The pornographic shop? The bookie joint? The gambling den? The discotheque dance hall? Would you think of looking in a pulpit? That is where you would find him. For, strange as it may seem, Satan is more concerned with what you think and what you believe than with what you do. Satan's desire is to control your mind so that he can control your actions. Satan does not spend his time in peripheral things; he concentrates his efforts on his goal, to control what you believe. Therefore Satan has moved into the pulpit.

Satan has a doctrine. It is referred to in I Timothy 4:1 where Paul writes: "The Spirit speaketh expressly that in the latter time some shall depart from the faith, giving heed to seducing spirits and doctrines of demons." And *doctrines of demons* does not refer to doctrines about demons but doctrines that are propagated by demons. In writing his letters to the seven churches, the Apostle John in Revelation 2:24 says, "I say unto the rest that are in Thyatira and as many as have not this doctrine, which hath not known the depths [or the deep things]of Satan, as they speak."

Preaching must stand as the most powerful influence to move and change men that this world has ever seen. Even with all the modern means of communication that Satan has at his disposal, there is no means of communication that can so change the course of a man's life or his conduct or his thinking as the divinely ordained means of preaching. One who has been called to preach has been called to control the minds of men. Satan will, of course, use every means at his disposal to change the thinking of an individual. He will use high pressure public relations tactics. He will use high pressure advertising through the printed page, radio, and television. But, when Satan had done that, he has still not claimed the most effective method that has ever been devised, which is preaching.

Therefore, to propagate his false doctrine, Satan occupies the pulpit in the guise of a minister of righteousness. He does this to dictate and to control what men believe. Satan's method of propagating his doctrine is described for us in II Corinthians 11: 13 where the Apostle writes: "Such are false apostles, deceitful workers, transforming themselves into the apostles of Christ. And no marvel, for Satan himself is transformed into an angel of light. Therefore it is no great thing if his ministers also be transformed as the ministers of righteousness, whose end shall be according to their works." Reading verse 14 a little differently, we see the emphasis that Paul intended: "Satan is transforming himself into an angel of light; therefore, it is no great thing if his ministers also are transforming themselves as the ministers of righteousness."

Satan, then, has a doctrine to propagate and he has a method of propagating it. And his method is to imitate God's method. He puts men in places where people will submit to their teaching. He gives to them the authority that belongs to a minister commissioned, instructed and sent by God. He then causes that deceiver to teach a false doctrine which will grip the minds and hearts of men. In I John 4:2 the Apostle emphasizes again this same fact: "Hereby know ye the Spirit of God. Every spirit that confesseth that Jesus Christ is come in the flesh is of God; and every spirit that confesseth not that Jesus is come in the flesh is not of God." In this passage you observe the apostle is warning his readers about the presence of false spirits. Now these false spirits are teachers, men who are representing themselves as men of God but who are energized by Satan. They come, not to propagate the truth of the Word, but to propagate the false doctrine that Satan wants to use to blind and bind the minds of men. And so there is a spirit that comes from God or a teacher who is sent by God; there is also an imitator of God's minister, one who comes with Satanic authority to deceive men.

Peter spoke of this same thing in II Peter 2:1: "There were false prophets among the people, even as there shall be false teachers among you who privily [or secretly, cleverly] shall bring in damnable heresies, even denying the Lord that bought them." These passages which we have brought together emphasize the fact that Satan works through men who pose as ministers of the gospel or as men of God, when in truth they are ministers of Satan, sent by Satan, with Satan's message to deliver.

Our Lord made it very clear that Satan will never propagate truth. Satan always propagates error. John 8:44 reads: "Ye are of your father, the devil." This was a strong statement because Christ was speaking to the religious leaders of His day. They were honorable, upright, educated, respected men who had been put in a position of authority because of their abilities in the religion of their day. But Christ said to them, "Ye are of your father, the devil." Christ called them that because when He came and said, "I am the Way, the Truth, and the Life," they said that that was a lie. They told men to follow their way, the way of conforming externally to the requirements of pharisaism. Christ said, "I am the Truth," and they said, "No, you are a liar; we have the truth. We got it from Moses." Christ said, "I am the Life," and they said, "No, you have life already because you are Abraham's physical seed. If you want to enter into fullness of life, pattern your life according to our traditions." They called Christ a liar. When Christ said, "I am the Son of God," they said, "You are a devil." They denied every word that came from the lips of the Lord Jesus. Therefore Christ said to them, "Ye are of your father the devil, and the lusts of your father ye will do. He was a murderer from the beginning and abode not in the truth, because there is no truth in him. When he speaketh a lie, he speaketh of his own for he is a liar, and the father of it." Christ was saying that Satan lied. You remember he lied when he came to tempt Eve, and he said to her: "Ye shall not surely die." But Christ is emphasizing more than that.

Satan not only lies, but he has the character of a liar. Satan had inaugurated a system which is false; it is contrary to the truth of God. And Satan is a liar not simply because he does not tell the truth; he is a liar because he has instituted a false system called "the deep things of Satan" that is contrary to the revealed truth of the Word of God. We find this emphasized in II Timothy 3:13 where Paul says, "Evil men and seducers [that is false teachers] shall wax worse and worse, deceiving, and being deceived." The false teachers, then, practice deception. Deluded and deceiving themselves, they speak delusion and deception to control the thinking of men.

In II Thessalonians 2, Paul emphasizes this again as he speaks concerning the coming of the lawless one. In verse 9 he writes, "Even him, whose coming is after the working of Satan with all power and signs and lying wonders, and with all deceivableness of unrighteousness in them that perish; because they received not the love of the truth, that they might be saved. And for this cause God shall send them strong delusion, that they should believe a lie."

What we are emphasizing as we gather these portions together is this: Satan has an avowed purpose, to control the thinking of men. If he can control their minds, he can then consequently control their actions. He has instituted a system of deception that goes counter to the revealed truth of God. He has transformed his ministers so that they appear as ministers of righteousness when, in truth, they are ministers of deceit, deception, and delusion. And he puts them in positions of authority and responsibility so that, as men give them respect because of their position, and submit to their teaching, they submit to the teachings of Satan and are brought under his delusion. Consequently their lives are conformed to his pattern.

In going through the Word of God, we find that there are certain specific areas of revealed truth which are the subject of Satanic attack. Certain doctrines of the Word of God Satan cannot and will not permit a man to believe if he can possibly deceive him or delude him. Satan will concede as much as he has to. If a man wants to respect Christ as a good teacher, Satan will concede. If a man wants to believe that the Bible is errant and fallible but it is a special book, Satan will concede. He will let a man hold as much of divine truth as the man insists on believing up to the point of certain basic essentials. And these Satan never has, never will, and never can concede.

The first doctrine that Satan opposes is the doctrine of the authority of the Scriptures, the doctrine of the verbal, plenary inspiration of the Word of God which gives authority and inerrancy to this Book. Perhaps some of these words are a little strange to you. When we say that the Word of God is verbally inspired, we mean that God's supervision of what was written extended to the individual words in the original text as given in the Scriptures. God did not give men ideas that they were then permitted to record in any generalization that pleased them. God's inspiration extended to the individual words. When we say that the Scripture is plenarily inspired, we mean that it is inspired in its entirety, from Genesis right through Revelation. While all Scripture may not have the same spiritual value, yet all is equally inspired of God. We may not get the same doctrine out of the book of Chronicles that we get out of the book of Ephesians, but Ephesians is no more inspired than the book of Chronicles. It is verbally inspired; it is inspired in its entirety.

Because God inspired the Scriptures, the Bible is without error. There is no geographical, no historical, no scientific, no religious, no doctrinal error to be found in the Book, because God would not be a party to deception by propagating error. And because the Word of God is given in its entirety by the Spirit of God and is without error, it is our absolute and final authority in all matters of life and doctrine. What we do and what we believe must be conformed to the Word of God or we are following the deception of Satan. This is a doctrine that Satan hates.

In II Timothy 4:4 we read that the day shall come when "they shall turn away their ears from the truth, and shall be turned unto fables." What is the truth? It is the Word of God. Satan's first purpose is to turn men away from belief in the integrity and authority of Scripture that rests upon its inspiration. Many have told me that they went to college or university with a simple faith in the Word of God that had been planted in their minds in childhood in some church that you refer to as the "old-fashioned kind." But as they were exposed to those educated men in whose classes they sat, they found that their attitude toward the Word of God was changing; and by the time their university course was over, they completely rejected the Scriptures considering them outmoded as a means of revelation and denying that they have any authority today. Those who so destroyed trust in the Word of God were instruments of Satan. They were his ministers posing as ministers of intellectual freedom, but they were doing his work. They were propagating his doctrine and taking away that which is the foundation of God's program. Satan cannot permit a man to accept the authority and integrity of the Word of God based on its inspiration. And to see how successful Satan has been in this part of his lie system, all you have to do is to investigate the average school in our country today dedicated to training ministers. It will be like searching for the proverbial needle in a haystack to find a school completely dedicated to the inspiration and the authority and integrity of the Word of God. Such schools are "ministers of righteousness," systematically destroying the foundation of truth. They are emissaries of Satan propagating his deception, his doctrine.

The second thing Satan cannot permit a man to accept is the doctrine of the Person of Christ. The Word of God presents Jesus Christ as the eternal Son of the eternal God. He is an uncreated one, equal with the Father, who to redeem us became flesh and took to Himself a true humanity, thus uniting the infinite God with a true and complete humanity so that we might have a Saviour to die on our behalf. God at the time of Christ's baptism certified the person of His Son by saying, "This is my beloved Son in whom I am well pleased." But there are those who do not hesitate to call God a liar and say that God was deceiving and deluding men. They teach that Jesus Christ was a good man, He was an honorable man, but He Himself was deluded and deceived. But they ask us to follow One who Himself was deluded, who thought that He was God but was not. It is this the Apostle John is warning about in I John 4:2: "Every spirit that confesseth that Jesus Christ is come in the flesh is of God; and every spirit that confesseth not that Jesus Christ is come in the flesh is not of God; this is that spirit of antichrist, whereof ye have heard that it should come; even now is already in the world." The Apostle, writing to that little flock where he ministered for so long, understood the deception of Satan. Satan who cannot permit man to accept the integrity of the Scriptures, likewise cannot permit man to accept the fact that God states that Jesus Christ is the eternal Son of the eternal God come in the flesh.

Along with this denial is the denial of the Virgin Birth of Christ. The only way God could come in the flesh was to come supernaturally, to come apart from a natural birth. The Old Testament promises that He would so come (Isaiah 7:14). The New Testament testifies that He came born of a virgin apart from a human father. If Jesus Christ is truly virgin born, there is no other explanation than that He is who God said He is, and what He claimed to be, the Son of God. So to do away with the deity of Christ, it is necessary for Satan to undermine the doctrine of the Virgin Birth of Christ. This is one of the doctrines of the Word of God most commonly attacked. It is being placarded across our newspapers continually that men in high positions publicly repudiate this doctrine, which is binding upon those who revere the Word of God. In so doing they are falling into the deception of Satan and have become his instruments even though they are garbed as ministers of righteousness. They are deceivers, and their deception is folly.

There is a third area which Satan cannot concede and will not under any circumstances permit man to believe. That is the doctrine of salvation based on the blood of Christ. If Satan hates the Word of God, and if Satan hates the doctrine of the Person of Christ, the deity of Christ, above all he hates the doctrine of the value of the shed blood of Christ. Peter infers this in II Peter 2:1: "There shall be false teachers among you, who privily shall bring in damnable heresies, even denying the Lord that bought them." Note that phrase, "denying the Lord that bought them." This brings us to the doctrine of redemption. *To redeem* means *to set free by purchasing*. And the purchase price according to the Word of God is the blood of Jesus Christ. And Christ died in order that we might be set free from the slave market of sin, that we might be delivered from bondage to sin, that we might be delivered from the guilt of sin, that we might be delivered from the penalty for our sins. The debt we owed to God was death because we had sinned. "For the wages of sin is death." Jesus Christ came to pay that debt, and He paid it in full. Jesus Christ did not bring God into a bankruptcy court where God settled for 10¢ on a dollar. When Christ came to pay our debt, He assumed it all. Since our debt was death, He shed His blood. And Satan hates the doctrine of the blood of Christ more than any other doctrine of the Word of God.

Now it is easy to see how Satan seeks to promote his doctrine. Our doctrine is based on the authority of Scripture. When Satan seeks to promote his doctrine, he sends one who poses as a minister of righteousness to substitute something for the place that belongs to the Word of God. Every false cult, sect and "ism" that exists has to supplement the Scriptures by some added book, which they claim is added revelation — whether it be *Science and Health With a Key to the Scriptures* by Mary Baker Patterson Glover Eddy, or whether it be the *Book of Mormon*, or whether it be the writings of Ellen G. White, or of Judge Rutherford and Pastor Russell, or whether it be Papal encyclicals, or whether it be the traditions of the fathers, the *Talmud*. In every false doctrine that is propagated, the Word of God has been superseded by writings of men which are then elevated to a position of authority over and above the Scriptures so that they become the basis of doctrine. So Satan sets the Word of God aside and substitutes the word of men. But it is the Word of God that reproves and rebukes and exhorts and convicts, and not any word that is penned by men. Therefore, when we go to men to bring them the truth of Scripture, we must confront them with the Word of God. It is the only thing that will do God's work.

When God presents a Person to be believed and followed, Satan's method is to set aside Jesus Christ and rob Him of the place of pre-eminence and focus attention on some other individual. And the vast proportion of the earth's population today

bows before some name other than the name of the Lord Jesus
Christ. Whether it be Mohammed or Buddha or Confucius or
some philosopher or some religious or political leader, it matters
little. Satan has done his work of capturing the minds of men by
bringing them into subjection to some authority other than Jesus
Christ. This danger pervaded the Corinthian church. The false
teachers who came into Corinth were not substituting another
gospel. But the Corinthian church was divided because the
teachers who came into the Corinthian church were elevated to
a position above the authority of Christ so that some men were
followers of Paul, some of Cephas, some of Apollos; and the
devilish work was done.

When Satan is face-to-face with the truth that men are saved
by faith in Jesus Christ, he has to substitute some other plan of
salvation. His ministers of righteousness substitute the ordinances,
persuading men that if they are baptized and take the Lord's
Supper and join a church, they will be saved. Or if they do
enough good deeds they will be saved. Or if they are charitable
and kind, they'll be saved. That is a Satanic deception, for the
truth of the Word of God is that stated by Peter, "There is none
other name under heaven given among men whereby we must
be saved," the name of the Lord Jesus Christ.

When Satan finds an individual who is committed to these
doctrines, who believes in the verbal plenary inspiration of Scripture and its integrity and authority, who believes that Jesus
Christ is the eternal Son of God, come in the flesh to redeem us,
believes that salvation is by faith in the blood of Christ alone,
does Satan leave him alone? Would to God it were true! Would
to God he would admit defeat! But Satan still continues to work
in one completely committed to these cardinal truths to so cloud
the issue that men are not confronted with the fact that salvation
is by grace through faith in Jesus Christ alone.

There are certain words that Satan hates, words like blood,
saved, born again. How easy it is, to ingratiate ourselves to an
individual, to leave these key words of the Gospel out of our
vocabulary as though we could sneak up on an individual on
his blind side and somehow lead them to faith in Christ without

telling them that they are sinners, and that they need to be saved, and they can be born again by faith in Jesus Christ. A person isn't saved because he has a nodding acquaintance with the man Jesus. He is saved because he personally receives the Lord Jesus Christ as his Saviour. He is not saved because he "makes a commitment to Christ"; he is saved because he receives Jesus Christ and trusts His blood for salvation. We can try to make the Gospel so relevant to unsaved men, we remove the offense of the cross. We don't want to say to men, "you are lost," because that will insult them. Of course it will. But no man will ever come to Christ unless he realizes he is lost. He'll never come to Christ unless he realizes he is under condemnation. Whereas the Word of God is supposed to be biting, we have pulled all the teeth and we are trying to masticate some people into salvation with toothless gums.

That isn't the way Paul did it. We need to be on guard lest Satan should gain an advantage over us. The Apostle in Galatians 5 has an interesting word in verse 11: "And I, brethren, if I yet preach circumcision, why do I yet suffer persecution? then is the offence of the cross ceased." May we put this in plain words? The cross is a stench in the nostrils of an unsaved man. We better beware about trying to use an atomizer so that what is an offense smells good lest people whom we may desire to reach with the Gospel should be deluded by Satan to believing that the issues are different from what they actually are. Christ said to Nicodemus, "Ye must be born again." You say "Men don't understand that term today." Maybe they don't, but it wouldn't take you two minutes to tell them what it means. "Men don't like to hear about blood." No, but men must be told that they need to be saved by blood. We who revere the Word as the Word of God, we who have respect for the authority of the Person of Christ, and are committed to the truth that salvation is by grace through faith based on the blood of Christ, should not try to make the Gospel so appealing to an unsaved man, that it cannot do its work, convicting, reproving, rebuking. If we do that, we have become tools of the evil one.

God loved the world, and sent His Son to save the world. God now sends believers into the world to tell men God's truth. And it must be presented in God's way with God's authority on God's terms so that men will realize they are lost and they need a Saviour, and that Jesus Christ is the only Saviour. The Gospel is the power of God that can redeem. The Gospel can bring a man low before God to recognize that he is lost, undone, and condemned. The Gospel can give forgiveness of sins and impart eternal life if it is presented in truth. We need to be on guard lest we permit our adversary inadvertently to use us as an instrument to pervert God's truth.

We say this final word to any of you who may never have received Christ as your personal Saviour. Perhaps you have been deceived and deluded by one of Satan's representatives. You have felt that the Scriptures had no authority, that Christ was just another good man, that you could work out your own salvation. On the authority of Scripture, there is only One who can save you and He is the Lord Jesus Christ. And He will save you the moment you say to Him, "I, a sinner, receive Christ as my personal Saviour." It is that simple but it is that final. Will you receive Him?

12

Satan's Response to the Preaching of the Word

Matthew 13:1 - 9

In the parable of the sower (Matthew 13) our Lord revealed Satan's activities when the Word of God is proclaimed. Hebrews 4:12 tells us that "the Word of God is quick [living] and powerful, and sharper than any two-edged sword, piercing even to the dividing asunder of soul and spirit, and of the joints and marrow, and is a discerner of the thoughts and intents of the heart." Satan knows that the Word of God is living and powerful. He knows, as you know, that it is the nature of that which is alive to reproduce itself. Live seed cannot lie dormant in the ground forever. Live seed, when allowed to remain in good soil and watered, will germinate and will grow and produce fruit. Since the Word of God is God's good seed, and it is living, the Word of God when sown on prepared soil will produce, and it will produce the peaceable fruit of righteousness.

This was the confidence of the prophet Isaiah when he wrote in Isaiah 55 that God will prosper the Word that is sown and will cause it to accomplish that for which God sends it forth. That was our Lord's teaching in Matthew 13, for He speaks in verse eight of seed that fell into good ground and brought forth fruit, some an hundredfold, some sixtyfold, and some thirtyfold. Lest the disciples miss the import of this teaching, our Lord explained in verse 23: "he that receiveth seed into the good ground is he that heareth the word and understandeth it; which also beareth fruit, and bringeth forth, some an hundredfold, some sixty, and some thirty." Our Lord affirms that, when the Word of God, the good seed, falls upon a heart that has been prepared by the

113

Spirit of God to receive that Word, there must be fruit. Since the Word of God is living, and dynamic or powerful, it will reproduce itself. Satan is fully conscious of that fact; and, whenever he anticipates that the Word of God will be preached, he is present to do his work of snatching the seed away. Satan, of course, would rather not have to do this work of taking away the seed that has been sown. He would rather so control the one who is doing the preaching that something other than the good seed of the Word of God is proclaimed.

Think of the work that Satan has to accomplish when the Word is preached: if there are 500 people present when the true Word of God is planted in 500 hearts, he has to have 500 demons to get into 500 different lives to take out that which has been sown. What an economy of operation it is if he can have those people who think they will be taught the Word of God hear some lie of the devil. He has had to work with only one individual instead of 500. But knowing that the Word of God will be proclaimed and that the truth of God will be declared, Satan has prepared to prevent the good seed of the Word from falling into the good ground so that it can bring forth fruit.

In the third verse of Matthew 13 our Lord has declared that a sower went forth to sow, and He explains that He Himself is the sower (Matthew 13:37). "He that soweth the good seed is the Son of Man; the field is the world; the good seed are the children of the kingdom." Through men whom Christ has redeemed, He now proclaims the Word of God, the good seed.

But as soon as the Son of God causes the seed of the Word to be sown, Satan and Satan's minions leap into action. We find in the fourth verse when He sowed, "some seeds fell by the wayside, and the fowls came and devoured them up." The wayside was the path along the edge of the field. At the edge of any man's field were set up marker stones. So as to lose no profitable soil, the path went along the boundary line. The soil was trodden down and was never plowed. In walking up and down the rows to scatter the seeds, some seed would fall upon that hard, packed pathway. There was no prepared soil that could receive it. When the seed fell on unprepared ground, birds followed the sower to snatch it away. Our Lord explained this part of His parable in verse 19: "When anyone heareth the Word of the kingdom, and understandeth it not, then cometh the wicked one, and catcheth away that which was sown in his heart. This is he which received seed by the wayside."

Two things are said about the good seed that fell along the wayside. First of all, it was not understood by the hearer. "He understandeth it not." The second thing said about this seed is that Satan removes the seed that was sown so that it cannot germinate. "The fowls came and devoured them up." Such seed cannot reproduce itself. This reveals to us the first of Satan's strategies in response to the preaching of the Word of God. First of all, when the Word of God is proclaimed, Satan will blind the mind so that the hearer does not understand what is spoken. When an individual hears a truth that he does not understand, he is ready and willing to surrender it. If Satan allows the seed to remain, that seed will germinate. The rains that fall from heaven will cause that seed to manifest its life; and, where there is life, there is always the possibility of fruit. Satan's first objective then is to remove the Word of God from your mind so that, when you hear it, you let it go in one ear and out the other. If you can dismiss the Word of God, and pay no attention to it, then Satan will have prevented it from being watered so that it can produce fruit. Satan will blind your mind to the truth of the Word of God if at all possible. Where there is no Word, there can be no growth, and where there is no Word, there can be no fruit. Fruit in the life of an individual is dependent upon reception of the Word of God because there can be no fruit apart from the living seed.

To keep you from receiving the Word of God, Satan will substitute something. If Satan sees you reach out to take this Book to get light for some present problem, he will substitute the word of a man who poses as a minister of the Gospel who will attempt to solve your problems apart from the Word of God. How many times in a quest for the truth concerning Jesus Christ have you read something from an individual, hoping to satisfy a spiritual thirst, but found it left you thirsty and did not satisfy? Why?

There was no life in it. It was not the seed of the Word of God. Satan will divert you from the Word of God if at all possible. There is nothing written, there is nothing spoken, that is seed other than the Word of God.

Or Satan will try to bring you to the place where the Word of God will be received with an unprepared heart and an unprepared mind. He will fill your mind with so much clutter that the Word of God cannot penetrate. Many find no profit by the Word that is taught in Sunday school or is preached Sunday morning because of what they did Saturday night. Satan begins his work to defeat the presentation of the Word long before it is preached. You didn't realize it. You thought you were having a time of entertainment or relaxation, not realizing Satan was preparing you to "hear" a sermon with deaf ears or heart.

Sometimes Satan will bring you to hear the Word with some unconfessed sin. Where there is unconfessed sin, the Spirit of God has to direct His attention to convicting, and He does not then do the work of teaching. The Spirit of God does not convict and teach at the same time. So if Satan can get you involved in some sin and bring you to where the Word of God will be preached with that sin unconfessed, Satan has made it impossible for you to understand and appropriate the Word of God. Unconfessed sin is part of Satan's program of putting seed along the wayside.

Or Satan will bring you into a congregation with some antagonism or some bitterness toward another believer that gets you occupied with that individual or yourself. That bitterness, that disunity prevents the Spirit of God from watering the seed that was sown to produce fruit to God's glory. Bitterness will so compact the soil of your heart that you are unreceptive to the Word of God.

There is a second response to the preached Word. We read in verse five: "Some fell upon stony places, where they had not much earth; and forthwith they sprung up, because there was no deepness of earth." Satan has to work a little harder with this individual. Satan couldn't prevent his hearing the Word of God. He hears it, he receives it and it is living seed because it begins to reproduce itself. Satan has to use another strategy. The seed has been sown, it has taken root, and is growing and ultimately will produce fruit unless its growth is arrested. What does Satan do? We read in the fifth verse that it is seed that falls among the "stony places." In verses 20 and 21 we have our Lord's explanation: "He that receiveth the seed into stony places, the same is he that heareth the word, and anon, with joy receiveth it; yet hath he not root in himself, but dureth for a while: for when tribulation or persecution ariseth because of the word, by and by he is offended." Here is an individual who hears the Word of God proclaimed and accepts it; he rejoices in it. This new-found love for the Word and the Lord whom the Word reveals leads him to tell another of his joy. But instead of having the same joyful response he had had, this individual looks at him with skepticism, with doubt, with amazement. And the Word of God that had begun to grow is stifled because of the opposition, the indifference, the doubt that is expressed when he seeks to share his faith in the Lord Jesus Christ. Our Lord told the disciples in the upper room that persecutions must come. Our Lord warned about civil persecution, political persecution, religious persecution, persecution that would come from within a family as well as persecution from without. He was seeking to prepare the disciples for this method of attack by the evil one.

How many individuals there are who have heard the Word of God, are convinced of its truth, and then turn back because they begin to count what it will cost them to stand unreservedly for Jesus Christ. How many businessmen there are who have never grown spiritually because they are afraid of what it will cost them in business life if they give themselves completely to Jesus Christ, and pattern their business according to His principles and obey Him above all else. How many young people there are who have veiled the fact that they believe the Scriptures are the Word of God because in school it may cost them something in the way of popularity or prestige. Thus the Word of God becomes unproductive because, after it begins to grow, persecutions come and stifle the growth.

Our Lord continues in verse seven: "Some fell among thorns,

and the thorns sprung up, and choked them." This is the third
method that Satan uses to remove the Word of God from the
life of an individual. Our Lord explains this in verse 22. "He
also that receiveth seed among the thorns is he that heareth the
word; and the care of this world, and the deceitfulness of riches,
choke the word, and he becometh unfruitful." Here is seed that
was planted on productive soil. It has even forced its way through
the briars so that it towers above them. Even though growing
in the midst of thorns, it is there. Satan has his hardest work yet,
for he has to root out a firmly-planted and well-grown plant.
How will he do it? Christ tells us in verse 22: by getting one
occupied with the cares or the responsibilities of this world and
by enticing with the deceitfulness of riches.

If Satan can't remove the Word before it germinates, or uproot
it when it is still a tender new shoot, if it has grown to the
point where it is ready to bear fruit, he will get us occupied with
material things. He will give some new objective in life that
supersedes the objectives and goals that we had from the Word
of God from Jesus Christ. Satan's method is to take a business-
man, for instance, and instead of demoting him as an act of
persecution (he tried that and it didn't work), he promotes him.
He elevates him to a position of prominence and authority to
the point that the man becomes too busy to have any time for
the Word of God. Such responsibility in his professional life occupies his time completely. Or Satan, who had tried to test a
man by poverty in his second method and found that that temptation only drove the individual to the Word of God for support,
will now reverse his tactics and make the man so rich that his
riches have become a snare. He becomes so enmeshed in pre-
serving and multiplying the things that have come to him that
he has no time for the Word of God. The cares of this world
get us occupied with ourselves and the deceitfulness of riches
gets us occupied with our material things. Either way, we become
so occupied with our position and station and responsibilities and
accomplishments in life that we neglect the Word of God. Where
the Word of God is neglected, there can be no fruit.

Perhaps you have thought that the material blessings you have came from God. May I say to you, they may be Satan's snare; they may be that which Satan is using in your life to root up the Word of God that is being preached so that there will be no fruit in your life. To repeat, Satan does not care what you do, but he is vitally concerned with what you believe and what you know. He's going to let you do anything that you want to do. But he cannot let you believe the Word of God and receive the Word of God and fashion your life according to the Word of God. To do so is to leave good seed in good soil that will be watered by the Spirit of God and which must produce its fruit in God's season.

It would be strange indeed if some of you, since you began to read, have not had your mind diverted to the business office, settling tomorrow's problems and clearing up yesterday's. Some of you housewives have been distracted by responsibilities at home. Do you think that is of the Spirit of God? No, the devil is buzzing around here as busy as the proverbial bee to keep some truth of the Word of God from being planted. Perchance you felt sleepy the last time you put yourself under a ministry of the Word. Do you think that was God's peace lulling you to sleep? No, there was something that would be good seed that Satan couldn't stand to have you hear so he put a temptation before you Saturday night. He persuaded you to stay up late and consequently you slept through the Sunday morning service. Satan looked at you while you were nodding and said, "That's one I don't have to worry about. No seed being planted there this morning." His work was being done.

In the first parable in Matthew 13 Christ taught what Satan does when the Son of God plants His seed. But that is only part of his work. In verse 24 our Lord told a second parable that is a counterpart of the first one. He said the "kingdom of heaven is likened unto a man which sowed good seed in his field; But while men slept, his enemy came and sowed tares among the wheat, and went his way. But when the blade was sprung up, and brought forth fruit, then appeared the tares also." The tare is a plant that looks so much like wheat that not until harvest time can you tell the difference between the two. The plants look alike but the tare never produces any grain. "So the servants of the householder came and said unto him, Sir, didst not thou sow good seed in thy field? from whence then hath it tares? And he said unto them, An enemy hath done this." Study our Lord's explanation in verse 36. This was a mystery to the disciples and they said, "Declare unto us the parable of the tares of the field. He answered and said unto them, He that soweth the good seed is the Son of Man; the field is the world; the good seed are the children of the kingdom; but the tares are the children of the wicked one; the enemy that sowed them is the devil; the harvest is the end of the world; and the reapers are the angels."

In our Lord's explanation He gives us the second response of Satan to the ministry of the Word. He is planting a counter-sowing to choke out the Word of God. We often overlook the fact that, while we submit ourselves for one or two hours a week to the preaching and teaching of the Word of God, we are subject to the sowing of Satan all the week long. And he is busy. One thing you can say about Satan is he's not lazy, and he will keep on with his sowing. And he's preparing the soil for his seed, so that it will bear his fruit. Every time you are turned away from the Word of God to the words of men, you are receiving his seed. Every time your mind is occupied with anything other than Jesus Christ, you are accepting the seed of Satan. Then you wonder why there is so little fruit in your life and so little growth in your Christian experience. There can be no growth apart from sowing of the good seed — no growth apart from the Word of God.

The Lord said in Matthew 13:8, "Some fell into good ground and brought forth fruit, some an hundredfold, some sixtyfold, some thirtyfold." He explained the basis of fruitfulness in verse 23, "He that received seed into the good ground is he that heareth the word, and understandeth it; which also beareth fruit, and bringeth forth, some an hundredfold, some sixty, some thirty." Notice that, in each instance, the seed was the same. That by the wayside, that on stony ground, that among thorns, it was all the same seed. In each instance the sower was the same, the Lord Jesus. So you cannot explain the difference in amount of

fruit by either the sower or the seed. There was only one difference and that was the preparedness of the soil. No preparation
— that which fell by the wayside. Scant preparation — that on
the stony ground. Little preparation — that which grew among
thorns. But there had been careful preparation in that which
produced an hundred and sixty and thirtyfold.

That which the Word of God produces in your life is directly
related to the preparation you have permitted the Spirit of God
to do in your life and heart. If you came to the Word with an
unprepared heart, the seed is taken away. If you came to the
Word with a life choked up with weeds, with sin, with bitterness,
with jealousy, with strife, the Word will never come to fruit.
But if you come to the Word of God with a life that has been
prepared to receive the truth of the Word by the Spirit of God,
the good seed sown by the Lord Jesus will produce its fruit.
As living seed, it must reproduce.

13

How Satan Tempts

Matthew 4:1 - 11

Satan's original rebellion challenged the authority of God. It challenged God's right to rule over His creation and His creatures, challenged God's right to be obeyed, challenged God's right to be believed. Through the unfolding drama of human history Satan has been perpetuating his lie, the lie that he has the right to rule, to be obeyed, to be believed. Ultimately the issue as to who has the right must be settled, for two cannot have authority in the same sphere. Two who hold divergent views cannot both be true. Two cannot claim the right to be worshiped. Satan recognized that he was a creature, that he possessed created life. Satan would have to acknowledge that God is creator and possessed uncreated life, but he sought to delay this direct confrontation. In the economy of God the time comes when the battle can no longer be postponed, when the conflict must be settled.

Before our Lord began His actual ministry He went out in the wilderness to challenge Satan, to compel Satan to do battle with Him to settle the issue once and for all. We have somehow come to the conclusion that Jesus Christ went out into the wilderness, that He was pursued there by Satan, that Christ was looking for some place to hide so that Satan might not find Him and challenge Him. Actually the converse is true. Satan was the pursued and Christ the pursuer; Christ, who had been listening for all the ages since Satan's rebellion to his claims, now compels Satan to meet Him in battle. Is God worthy to be obeyed? Is His Word worthy to be trusted? Is God worthy to be worshiped? Satan, knowing the ultimate outcome of this conflict between himself and Christ, certainly sought to flee from the place of temptation. Christ was in the wilderness under the Spirit's control; He was there in the will of God. He was there to pursue the Accuser and to compel the Accuser to put Him to test. In the record given to us in Matthew 4 we find the temptation of Jesus Christ by His adversary.

According to the Word of God there are only three channels, or gates, through which Satan can gain access to the citadel of a man's life. Satan can enter through the lust of the flesh, through the lust of the eyes, or through the pride of life. The writer to the Hebrews tells us that Christ was tested in all points like as we are, yet without sin (Hebrews 4:15). The writer is not suggesting that Christ was subjected numerically to every testing with which we have been tested but he is asserting that Jesus Christ was tested through every channel. Every gate was assaulted which Satan could possibly attack in order to conform Christ to the will of Satan. It is therefore significant to note that Christ's testing was in three specific areas. When tested as to the lust of the flesh, He hungered. The pride of life tested His faith in God. As to the lust of the eye, all of the kingdoms of the world were shown to Him in a moment of time. We are familiar with the record that is given to us of Christ's temptations. Let us notice these areas as they reveal to us Satan's method of temptation today. Satan's manner of dealing with Christ and his method for you are one and the same.

It is recorded in Matthew that Christ went into the wilderness to do battle with Satan, not according to His own will but according to the will of God, for He was led by the Spirit into the wilderness. He went not in His own strength or power, but, consciously dependent upon the sustaining power of the Holy Spirit. He went not to seek His own things, but to settle the issue that was raised by Satan's original rebellion against God. The Scripture records that for forty days and forty nights our Lord went without physical food. It was not until that extended period of time had terminated that Jesus Christ felt physical hunger. Matthew makes this very clear when he says He had fasted forty days and forty nights and "he was *afterward* an hungered."

There is no natural explanation as to how a man could continue for this extended period of time without physical food and feel no adverse effects. Yet this is explained to us in the fourth chapter of John's gospel. During Christ's visit to Samaria, in order that He might have time alone with one in deep spiritual need, He sent the disciples into the village to obtain food. While the disciples were gone our Lord met the spiritual need of the Samaritan woman. He revealed Himself to her as the One who had come from God in order to satisfy the needs of men. After our Lord had concluded His time with her, the disciples returned to Him bringing the food that they had purchased in the city. They invited Him, saying, "Master, eat" (John 4:31). But He said unto them, "I have meat to eat that ye know not of. Therefore said the disciples one to another, Hath any man brought him ought to eat? Jesus saith unto them, My meat is to do the will of him that sent me, and to finish his work." Our Lord revealed to the disciples on that occasion that His relationship to the will of God was that which sustained Him hour by hour and day by day. As other men depended upon physical food to sustain their bodies, He was dependent upon the will of God to sustain Him. As He walked in dependence upon God and in perfect obedience to the will of God, God sustained Him in that which God had for Him to do. Our Lord went for forty days and forty nights without physical food and was sustained during that period because He was in a place of perfect obedience to the will of God. His dependence upon the Spirit of God while in a place of obedience to God gave Him the sustenance that His body needed.

It was in the very area of His relationship to the will of God that Satan came with his first test. Satan assumed the truth of the Person of Christ. In your English text you read Satan's words, "*If* thou be the Son of God." We need not remind you that the Scriptures tell us that the demons believe and tremble (James 2:19). While modern man does not hesitate to deny the doctrine of the deity of Jesus Christ, and does not hesitate to deny that

Jesus Christ is the eternal Son of the eternal God come in the flesh through the virgin birth, no angel of hell has ever yet questioned the Person of Jesus Christ. Satan on this occasion is not questioning the doctrine of the Person of Christ; he is assuming it. This might properly be read, "Since thou art the Son of God, command that these stones be made bread." God had given food to sustain the body. That was made very clear at the time of creation, for when God placed Adam and Eve in the garden, He said to His creatures, "Of every tree of the garden thou mayest freely eat" (Genesis 2:16). God's method of sustaining the body was through the consumption of food. Satan then is not tempting Christ to do something that the Word of God had forbidden. Christ was being tested in an area which God had commanded and approved. Thus in a perfectly reasonable, logical way, Satan came to Christ and said, "Since you are the Son of God, command these stones that they be made bread."

Satan was recognizing what men today are not willing to recognize. Men today cast doubt on the authority of the Word of God. For instance, the Word says that all things that exist were created by Him. The Word of God teaches that the universe came into existence by the power of the Lord Jesus Christ. The Word reveals that Jesus Christ is the Son of God. Modern man does not hesitate to call the Word of God false and to pronounce God a liar. But Satan is not as bold as some men are. He acknowledged that Jesus Christ was the Creator and the Son of God and by the spoken word He could perform again the miracle that He had performed at the time of creation. It would be far simpler for Jesus Christ to transform a stone into bread than to call this universe into existence out of nothing, and Satan acknowledged that Jesus Christ could do it. So he challenged Him: Command these stones to be made bread."

Wherein, then, is the temptation? God has given food to sustain the body. Christ, after a period of forty days fasting was in need of physical sustenance. Jesus Christ had the power and the authority to command stones to make them into bread. Where is the temptation? The subtle temptation which Satan put before Jesus Christ was the temptation to depart from the will of God.

Since Jesus Christ was in the wilderness under the control of the Spirit and was being sustained by His obedience to the Spirit of God, the physical hunger that He endured was part of God's will for Him. The hunger was a part of God's design. For Jesus Christ to exercise an independent power to meet His own needs was to disobey the will of God as it was revealed to Him.

The subtlety of Satan's suggestion was this: Since you are a Son of God, it is unreasonable that you should be asked to deny yourself anything that you want. His suggestion is that Sonship permits independence of God. Since you are a Son, why do you have to deny yourself anything? Meet your own need without continuing in the will of God, without being dependent upon the Father. The first thing that Satan wanted of Christ then was for Christ to disobey and to depart from the place of perfect obedience to the will of God.

Obedience is what God wants of us. God has a plan for us and His plan is made known in the Word. God has revealed it with remarkable clarity so that one who turns to the Scriptures can know step-by-step what God has for him, what God expects of him, what God's will is for him. We have somehow come to feel that the sonship which we have because we belong to Jesus Christ gives us the right to sit in judgment upon the will of God — to decide whether we will submit to the will of God or not, to continue in our own way if it pleases us, to ignore the commands of Scripture when it suits us, to do as we please. Satan comes with the subtle suggestion that, since you are a son because of your faith in Jesus Christ, you don't have to do what He says. You have rights as a son. You have a mind of your own; use it. Satan's first temptation to Christ was to depart from the will of God for Him. That is Satan's first great desire for you; that you should ignore the will of God and become independent.

The second temptation is recorded in Matthew 4:5, 6. Satan took Christ "into the holy city [Jerusalem] and setteth him on a pinnacle of the temple, and saith unto him, If thou be the Son of God, cast thyself down; for it is written, He shall give his angels charge concerning thee: and in their hands they shall bear thee up, lest at any time thou dash thy foot against a stone." The city of Jerusalem was built on the top of a hill, and around the city was a thick, high wall built for protection. The corner of the city wall of Jerusalem was some 400 feet above the floor of the valley of the Kidron below. Jesus Christ was placed by Satan there on the edge of the city wall, known even to the present day as "the pinnacle of the temple." Satan directed his gaze downward into the valley some 400 feet below and said to Christ, "You quoted the book of Deuteronomy by which you turned aside my first temptation, 'Man shall not live by bread alone, but by every word that proceedeth out of the mouth of God.' Your reply shows me that you have confidence in what God has said. Now I want to see just how much confidence you actually have. Let me quote a promise to you: The psalmist said 'He shall give his angels charge concerning thee and they shall bear thee up in their hands lest at any time thou dash thy foot against a stone.' Now if you believe the Word of God as you say you do, then jump and demonstrate your faith. Challenge God, put God to the test and see if God is to be trusted. Demonstrate your faith in the promise of God."

This, like the first temptation, sounds quite reasonable and logical. If we have the Word of God and we have discovered a pertinent promise from the Word of God, we have a right to claim it; we can rest upon it. After all, what guarantee do we have that God has forgiven us our sins when we believe in Jesus Christ as a personal Saviour? We have nothing but the Word of God. What assurance do we have that there is no condemnation, no judgment, to those that are in Christ Jesus? We have nothing but the promise of the Word of God. Our whole destiny rests upon the trustworthiness of the Word of God. We who have received Jesus Christ have entrusted our eternal destiny to the Word of the Father; is it to be trusted? So Satan suggested that Jesus Christ put God to the test.

Behind this was the subtle temptation to doubt the Word of God. It had been written, "God shall give his angels charge over thee," but that promise was to those who were in obedience to God's will, to those who were walking according to the Word of God. For Jesus Christ to put God to the test was to say that He would not accept the fact simply because God said it, but only if He demonstrated it for Himself.

The scientist who says, "I will believe what I can prove in my laboratory," is basically a skeptic. He puts himself in the place of a judge and demands that he be satisfied. When God has made a statement and we put it to a test, we say in effect that we don't believe God. Satan came to Christ and tempted Him to demonstrate how great His faith was in what God said He would do. Christ replied by saying, "Thou shalt not tempt the Lord thy God (v. 7)." Jesus Christ did not have to put God to a test to believe Him. Jesus Christ believed God. An individual who puts God's Word to the test is saying that he won't believe Him until He does something to prove Himself. That is the test of the devil! If you try to prove it, you are calling God a liar. That is exactly what Satan wants you to do. You are succumbing to Satan's second test in which Satan's desire is to lead you to doubt the Word of God.

When Christ would not succumb to Satan's second temptation, he put a third before Him. We read in the eighth verse of Matthew 4: "The devil taketh him up into an exceeding high mountain, and showeth him all the kingdoms of the world, and the glory of them; and saith unto him, All these things will I give thee, if thou wilt fall down and worship me." Authority over the earth was deposited by the Creator in the hand of Adam, and he as God's appointed ruler administered God's authority over the earth. When Adam and Eve succumbed to Satan's temptation and ate of the forbidden fruit, they surrendered the scepter that God had given them into the hand of Satan, and Satan became the god of this world. Satan has existed as a usurping ruler from the time of Adam's fall to the present time. It was God's purpose as stated in Psalm 8 that He should wrest the scepter from Satan and restore it to Jesus Christ, the Son of Man, that He might rule as King of kings and Lord of lords. Satan, knowing that he had the authority of an usurper, showed Jesus Christ the glory of the kingdoms of this earth. At that moment he offered to release the scepter that he held in his hand to turn it over to Jesus Christ so that He might reign as a King over kings and Lord over lords. There was one condition: that Jesus Christ should worship him.

The subtlety of this temptation was that the One who has the right to be worshiped also has the right to be obeyed. If Jesus Christ should give Satan one act of worship, reasonably and logically He must obey the one whose right to receive worship he had just acknowledged. Satan's desire was to divert the worship that belongs to God to himself. This was the climactic temptation that Satan put before Christ. He invited Him to disobey the will of God and to doubt the Word of God, but those were all incidental to this great desire: to divert the worship that belongs to God to himself.

On the authority of the Word of God, this is what Satan wants from you more than anything else. When Jesus Christ stood in the upper room a week after His resurrection, He showed the disciples His hands and His side and Thomas burst forth with the words, "My Lord and my God." Satan wants to hear those words from the lips addressed to himself more than anything in this world. He is willing to surrender any claim that he makes to this universe if he can get you to worship him and to submit to him, to obey him and to do his will. If you acknowledge Satan's right to be worshiped, you have conceded his right to be obeyed. Satan works upon your mind and upon your heart and upon your will to bring you to the place that you will listen to him and say, "Yes, my lord." When he has brought you to that place, he then looks up toward the face of God and says, "Here is one more who says that I am god, that I have the right to be obeyed, who recognizes my authority instead of yours."

The world has walked in disobedience. The world, by submitting to Satan's authority, has echoed Satan's claim that God ought to be deposed and that Satan ought to be enthroned. It was not until Jesus Christ came into this world that there was One who obeyed the will of God perfectly. When Christ in the garden of Gethsemane said to the Father, "Not my will but thine be done," He was saying in effect to the Father, "Satan claims the right to be obeyed, to be believed, and to be worshiped. The human race has echoed his claim, but I submit to You in order that the world and angels might know that Thou art God; beside Thee there is no other and Your will is to be obeyed and Your Word believed and Your Person worshiped."

God's desire for you is that you should obey His will, that you should believe His Word, and that you should worship His Person just as Jesus Christ did. You can be an object lesson for God to the angels through your submission, through your faith, through your worship that He is God and beside Him there is no other.

How easy it is to disobey, to doubt and to withhold the sacrifice of praise and thanksgiving that rightly belongs to God. We challenge you in the light of the Word of God to examine your walk in relation to the will of God, your heart's attitude toward the Word of God and to the Person of the Father, lest you fulfill the desire of Satan.

14

Satan's Steps in Temptation

I John 2:7 - 17

Many of God's children have been deceived into believing that Satan is invincible and that when he tempts a man there is nothing the individual can do to withstand him; that he has so many devices at his disposal that, whether we desire it or not, eventually he must triumph over us. This is a lie of the Devil. It is a lie designed to blind us to the steps which Satan uses in temptation. For if we understand these steps and are on guard against them, if we understand the devices of the evil one, we are prepared to meet him and by the Spirit's help to defeat him.

The Apostle Peter in I Peter 5:8 says, "Your adversary, the devil, as a roaring lion, goeth about seeking whom he may devour." Satan roars to attract attention to himself and to distract us from the true nature of his devices. John, in I John 2:16, writes concerning the avenues through which Satan can assault an individual. It is a comfort to know that Satan cannot attack through a multitude of channels but can attack the individual through only three. These and only these three are the gates through which Satan can enter into the life of an individual. They are well-known. The Apostle John writes that all that is in the world can be summarized under three categories: the lust of the flesh, the lust of the eyes, and the pride of life. All sin, of necessity, falls into one of these three classifications. There is that which is fleshly, or carnal. This division recognizes that man, because of Adam's sin, is possessed of a nature that is characterized by its fleshliness, by its appetite, its desires, its cravings, its passions. Satan may appeal to these sins of the flesh.

The second category of sin, which also characterizes the nature of man, is referred to in the phrase, "the lust of the eye." This reveals the fact that man is not only carnal by nature but also basically selfish; that what he sees he desires and covets and what he desires or covets he will attempt to attain for himself. This may be in a realm widely separated from the realm of the flesh. Man is covetous or selfish by nature and Satan may lead man away in temptation through this basic selfishness.

The third category of sins characteristic to human nature is found in the phrase, "the pride of life." There are those sins that appeal to pride because the human nature is basically proud; it loves and strives for that which promotes and elevates the individual, pleases the individual, gives a sense of independence to the individual.

When Satan comes to tempt an individual, he must appeal to one of these three basic characteristics of the human nature, its carnal capacity, its selfish interests, or its pride. Satan is not concerned only in having an individual receive a temptation and consider that temptation. Satan is concerned with having him succumb to that temptation; he is directing his temptations ultimately to the will of the individual to produce an act or a thought or a word which is contrary to the revealed will of God. He may use the mind, or he may use the heart, or a combination of these two. But ultimately his desire is to produce an act that comes from the will of the individual who submits to the enticements of Satan and follows him in disobedience against God. Satan recognizes that what a man knows he comes to love and what a man loves he will obey. So Satan plants a seed in the mind and then generates that seed so that affection for that thing is produced, since what a man loves ultimately he will serve. This process may be spread over an extensive period of time. A seed may be planted and then left over a long period until a man eventually comes to love what Satan has proposed and then finally obeys Satan's bidding. Or, the process may be speeded up so that love for that thing which Satan has planted in the mind may be almost instantaneous. But the one object is to produce obedience to that which Satan desires. An individual facing any temptation can analyze it to discover immediately into which category it falls. Is it an appeal to the lust of the flesh? Is it an appeal to the basic selfish nature through the lust of the eyes? Or is it an appeal to pride? When one determines the nature of the attack he then can use the Word of God, energized by the Spirit of God, to meet that attack.

In the wilderness temptations previously cited, Christ used the Word of God to resist Satan's attacks. In the area of appeal to the lust of the flesh, He replied from the Word, "Man shall not live by bread alone, but by every word of God." In the second area, through the lust of the eyes, He met the temptation with: "Thou shalt worship the Lord thy God, and him only shalt thou serve." In response to this appeal to selfishness Christ said, "I am willing to wait God's time." To Satans appeal to pride, Christ again quoted from the Word of God, "Thou shall not tempt [or put to the test] the Lord thy God." Then we read in Luke 4:13 "when the devil had ended all the temptation. . . ." When Satan had appealed to the lust of the flesh, and to the lust of the eyes and to the pride of life there was no other channel through which he could seek to approach the Lord Jesus Christ. Satan had no other devices to tempt Christ than those which he has used so successfully in the life of every man from the time of Adam's sin to the present time. Christ's victory came because He recognized the nature of the appeal and then could use the appropriate Scripture to resist that temptation. You will notice this was not a blind adherence to the Word of God. Christ, by analyzing and understanding the temptation, was able to apply a specific principle and promise of the Word of God to that temptation. Many of us go down in defeat before Satan, not because we don't respect the Word of God, for we do, but we are ignorant of what is in the pages of the Word of God and we are unable to apply a specific word to a given situation. This is what Christ did.

In II Samuel 11 we read of one who was tested by the evil one who did not triumph. David's sin is written across the pages of the Word of God to remind us of the peril that faces the child of God who does not discern Satan's method of attack and then use scriptural principles to resist. King David was cooling himself upon his housetop in the evening of the day. We read in the second verse, "It came to pass in an eveningtide, that David arose from off his bed, and walked upon the roof of the king's house: and from the roof he saw a woman washing herself; and the woman was very beautiful to look upon. David sent messengers, and took her; and she came in unto him, and he lay with her. . . ." We notice in the second verse that Satan's first attack on David was through the lust of the eyes, for he looked and saw. Because he was basically selfish, as all men are, he coveted what he saw. He could rationalize with himself and say that as king he had absolute authority over all his subjects, and it was a royal prerogative to requisition that which the king desires.

But the Word of God was very specific. The law said, "Thou shalt not commit adultery." He had further instruction given in Deuteronomy 17. There, as Moses was preparing Israel to become a self-governing nation, he anticipated that God one day would give Israel a king. Moses said in verse 14, "Thou shalt say I will set a king over me, like as all the nations, that are round about me; Thou shalt in any wise set him king over thee, whom the Lord thy God shall choose: one from thy brethren shalt thou set king over thee: thou mayest not set a stranger over thee, which is not thy brother. But he shall not multiply horses to himself, nor cause the people to return to Egypt, to the end that he should multiply horses: forasmuch as the Lord hath said unto you, Ye shall henceforth return no more that way." Men will trust in might, in power, in self-defense and will not cast themselves in dependence upon God, so God said the king shall not build a great stable of horses. Verse 17, "Neither shall he multiply wives to himself, that his heart turn not away: neither shall he greatly multiply to himself silver and gold."

That which David was contemplating was forbidden, not only by the law but by the added specific instructions of the Word of God. But David looked and what he saw he coveted, because he was basically selfish. Then that which David saw and lusted after he sent for. The lust of the eyes promoted lust of the flesh, and he put a plan into operation to gain that which the flesh coveted. That which he saw and desired, he took. The mind saw, then the heart lusted, and then the will disobeyed the Word of God.

The steps of temptation that carried David to disgrace are the steps that Satan uses in the experience of every man to bring that individual out of the will of God and to obedience to himself.

We find that the Word of God gives some specific instructions because of the three steps in temptation. In Philippians 4:8 the Apostle speaks concerning the mind, "Finally, brethren, whatsoever things are true, whatsoever things are honest, whatsoever things are just, whatsoever things are pure, whatsoever things are lovely, whatsoever things are of good report; if there be any virtue, and if there be any praise, *think on these things.*" Again in II Corinthians 10:5 the Apostle says we are to " . . . cast down imaginations, [that is: bring under judgment every wicked thought] and every high thing that exalteth itself against the knowledge of God, and bringing into captivity every thought to the obedience of Christ."

Satan begins with the mind. He plants a desire in that mind whether through the flesh or through selfishness or through pride. The Word of God says that that seed which Satan has planted is to be uprooted before it germinates, before it proceeds a step further, for if that thought planted by Satan is allowed to remain in the mind it will bear its fruit. So when Satan attacks through the mind that thought is to be judged, to be recognized as a satanic approach. It must be recognized as a first step in temptation and uprooted by the Word of God and by the power of the Spirit so it is not allowed to remain to produce sin.

In the second place, Satan moves from the mind to the area of the heart. That which he has planted in the mind that appeals to the lust of the flesh or the lust of the eyes or the pride of life becomes the object of your affections. That is why Solomon who had great experience in wrestling with Satan, usually to his own destruction, wrote in Proverbs 4:23, "Keep [or guard] thy heart with all diligence; for out of it are the issues of life." If that seed planted in the mind is allowed to begin to germinate, the heart will start loving what Satan has put there. That is why the Apostle has to command us in I John 2:15, "Love not the world, neither the things that are in the world." James has to remind us that to love the world is to become an adulterer against God because the world is no friend of God (James 4:4).

A man needs to examine not only his mind to keep it cleansed, but to examine his affections. What a man knows and loves he ultimately will obey unless that progress is interrupted by the Word of God and the Spirit of God. In I Samuel 15:22, Samuel reminds Saul that to obey is better than sacrifice. If a man has received a temptation to his selfish, proud, carnal nature and he begins to love it, the next step is to obey it. The affections must be purified lest we serve sin.

In writing Romans 13:14 Paul gave us a summary principle that is of paramount importance, "Put ye on the Lord Jesus Christ, and make not provision for the flesh, to fulfil the lusts thereof." Because we are prone to put ourselves in situations where we subject ourselves to Satan's attack, we simplify his work. Paul warns the child of God against opening his mind so that Satan can pour thoughts into it. He warns the child of God against opening his heart so that Satan can stir emotions within it. He also warns the individual against making himself subject to Satan's temptations. Much that we read, much that we see, much that we do is diametrically opposed to Paul's principle of Romans 13:14, and we are filling our minds with that which Satan can use. We are subject to Satan's attacks because we make provision for the flesh. Satan moves in on that which we have put there because we did not heed Paul's admonition. We have allowed our affections to be diverted from the Lord Jesus Christ and have come to love the things of this world so that Satan's work is already partly done; he can move in on the affections for which he is not responsible but which we have generated. Then we wonder why we are under such an attack from the evil one. It is not his doing. He is only taking advantage of what we have provided him to work with. It is a short step from disobedience to this principle to falling into sin. Make no provision for the flesh to fulfill the lusts thereof.

Satan cannot attack you in an infinite number of ways; he must appeal in only three ways: he must appeal to that which is fleshly, that which is selfish, or that which is the manifestation of pride. The Word of God gives us this instruction that we might understand the nature of the temptation and meet it through the Word and through the Holy Spirit. We need to safeguard our minds and hearts so that we are not providing that which Satan can use to produce sin.

15

How Satan Operates

Matthew 17:14 - 21

Many of God's children live a defeated life because they do not recognize the nature of the adversary and the kind of conflict in which they are engaged. Our adversary is so cleverly and subtly camouflaged many do not even recognize his existence. There can be no victory until we recognize the nature of the war. It was this fact Paul emphasized in Ephesians 6:12. "We wrestle not against flesh and blood, but against principalities, against powers, against the rulers of the darkness of this world, against spiritual wickedness in high places." We fight an unseen adversary, but though he is unseen, he is powerful and formidable.

We recognize that Satan as a created being is not omnipresent. Although the angels are supernatural, they are not gods and they cannot be everywhere present as God is. The angels as personal beings did not lose their personality in the fall with Satan. Nor did Satan lose his personality because of the fall. The limitations placed upon Lucifer by creation continue as his limitations after his fall, for Satan's rebellion did not give him prerogatives that belong to God. So Satan cannot be everywhere present at one time, warring against God and against God's children. Satan has to operate through those angels that followed him in his original rebellion.

Scripture has little to say concerning the extent of the angelic rebellion. What Scripture does infer is that when Satan rebelled a great host of created angelic beings followed him, and those who accepted his leadership and rebelled with him are referred

138

to as demons. This word in the King James text is translated *devils*, but should more properly be translated *demons*.

In Ephesians 6:12 Paul tells us that Satan has followed the pattern of God's arrangement and has ordered his demons into different hierarchies called principalities and powers and rulers. To each of these hierarchies is assigned a different responsibility. Scripture does not tell us the responsibilities assigned to these different groups. We do know that they have one common purpose: to oppose God and to defeat God's program for men in the earth as that purpose is revealed in the Scriptures.

In Revelation 9:11 there is another reference to this organization of the demonic world where we find in the first ten verses that innumerable demons have been released from the abyss which is the destiny of all the fallen angels. They are released into the earth to inflict suffering and torture upon men. In verse 11 it is recorded that "they had a king over them which is the angel of the bottomless pit whose name in the Hebrew tongue is Abaddon and in the Greek tongue hath his name Apollyon." Apollyon or Abaddon means *one who exterminates*. Thus we find that the demons are organized under the leadership of one who bears the name, *One who exterminates*. Under his leadership these demons will be released in order that they might exterminate the purpose or plan of God.

We know nothing of the numerical extent of the demons. We know that each individual who has ever lived had a guardian angel. The Word of God makes this very clear. The original extent of the angelic creation evidently far exceeded the total number of all individuals who ever have lived or ever will live upon the face of the earth. It would seem a valid conclusion that the rebels organized under Satan equal or exceed in number the number of the total population of the earth at any given time from Adam to the end-time.

Evidently the demons don't like men. Scriptures seem to infer that when given any choice they shun the scenes of human habitation. Christ, in Matthew 12:43, speaks concerning demonic activity, "The unclean spirit that is gone out of a man, he walketh through dry places, seeking rest, and findeth none." When a man was delivered from demonic control, the demon went out into the desert or the wilderness to flee the place of human habitation. Isaiah 13 refers to this fact again in symbolic language, where in verse 20 he speaks of the city of Babylon that will be destroyed, "It shall never be inhabited . . ." and in verse 21, "But wild beasts of the desert shall lie there; and their houses shall be full of doleful creatures; and owls shall dwell there, and satyrs shall dance there." And in this symbolic language Isaiah says that this place which had once been a center of world empire would be destroyed and left uninhabited and would then become a dwelling place of demons.

Certainly demons are uncomfortable living around an individual who knows Christ as a personal Saviour or in an area where God is recognized and His authority honored. That is why we see less of demonic activity in our country than would be evident in many places in the world. If you have talked much with missionaries you know that as they go to heathen lands that are utterly blind to the Gospel and to the truth of the Word of God, they are impressed with the fact that they are surrounded by evil demonic influences and they live under the pressure of that demonic presence. While they are in a heathen land they are especially subject to satanic attack because they are invading a territory occupied and possessed by the enemy, and he resists their presence. One of the principal reasons that we need to be faithful in praying for our missionaries is that they have gone into the center of the enemy's camp to defeat the adversary. You may be certain that they will be subject to all sorts of attacks by the enemy to nullify their testimony, to defeat them spiritually, to destroy their physical health and strength so that they cannot minister, to surround them with countless dangers to prevent their ministry from coming to fruition. The absence of the Gospel leaves an area subject to satanic control in a very real way.

One of the devices of Satan has been to blind us to the extent of this demonic activity, to delude us into believing that there is no such person as Satan and no such persons as demons. If we deny their existence we are not engaged in a warfare against them. We leave ourselves open to their attack, and they may defeat or destroy us with ease. While many people are willing to concede the existence of angels, they do not recognize that demons are real personalities and exercise any influence in our lives at all. Satan would like us to believe that such a doctrine is the product of medieval superstition and has no place in an enlightened twentieth century mind. That is a device of Satan to camouflage his existence in our midst and his attack and influence on our lives so that we will not be walking in Christian victory.

The Word of God has much to say about demons. If we were not basing our doctrine upon the Word of God we would be most foolish indeed to venture into this realm. Yet we have the revelation of the Word of God concerning these facts and truths. In I Kings 22 you see the interesting fact that Satan through demonic activity can control governments and movements in the political realm. God has a purpose for this earth; that is to set His Son, Jesus Christ in a place of authority as King of kings and Lord of lords. It is God's purpose to subdue all kingdoms and tongues and nations to the authority of Jesus Christ. That plan is under constant attack by Satan who seeks to control governments and move governments away from the recognition of the authority of God to bring them into subjection to his authority so that he may exercise world-wide dominion. Many who follow the front pages of the newspapers today would agree that Satan has done a good job.

In I Kings 22 is an illustration of how Satan works in the political realm. Verse 20 reads, "The Lord said, Who shall persuade Ahab, that he may go up and fall at Ramoth-gilead? . . . " It was God's purpose to judge the wicked king, Ahab, by having him fall in battle. Now to have Ahab fall in battle he must have an adversary and a nation must decide to move against Israel. So the question is asked how this could be arranged. "One said in this manner and another said in that manner. And there came forth a spirit, and stood before the Lord, and said, I will persuade him. And the Lord said unto him, Wherewith? And he said, I will go forth, and I will be a lying spirit in the mouth of all his prophets. And he said, Thou shalt persuade him, and prevail also: go forth, and do so."

Without going into all of the ramifications of this passage we see that an evil spirit or a demon spoke to Ahab through his false prophets and Ahab listened to the false prophets instead of listening to the true prophet of God and Ahab followed the false prophets. When the false prophets said he would be victorious, it was a lie. By accepting the falsehoods of Satan, Ahab went into battle and was defeated, and he lost his life. Demons moved in the political realm. The purpose of overthrowing Ahab was to prevent David's Son from coming to David's throne to rule as King of kings and Lord of lords.

The demons work, not only in the political realm by moving heads of state; they also work in the religious realm. Several Scriptural passages recognize this. In Leviticus 17 the people were going through outward forms of religion, offering the sacrifices according to what was prescribed in the law of Moses, but in verse 7 God said: "They shall no more offer their sacrifices unto demons." In Deuteronomy 32:17 this same fact is inferred, that when an individual offers a sacrifice to an idol he is offering sacrifices to demons. In I Timothy 4:1 Paul says, "The spirit speaketh expressly, that in the latter times some shall depart from the faith, giving heed to seducing spirits, and doctrines of demons" — the doctrines that are being propagated by demons. Behind every idol that has ever been erected to become a center of worship was a demon, and demons propagate all of the false religions and the forms of idolatry that ever have or ever will exist. This is a part of Satan's deception. He works in the religious realm to prevent men from coming under the authority of God that they might continue under the authority of Satan.

The Gospels contain the greatest number of references to demonic activity. This demonic activity was so prevalent because the Son of God was personally present among men. When He was offering Himself as a Saviour and Sovereign, Satan and his minions were whipped into a frenzy of activity in order that they might oppose Him and defeat Him. Several references will suffice here. In Mark 1:23-26 we read that when Christ came into Capernaum there was ". . . a man with an unclean spirit [a demon]; and he cried out, Saying, Let us alone; what have we to do with thee, thou Jesus of Nazareth? art thou come to destroy us? I know thee who thou art, the Holy One of God. And Jesus rebuked him, saying, Hold thy peace and come out of him. And when the unclean spirit had torn him, and cried with a loud voice, he came out of him. And they were all amazed." Christ stood there to present Himself as the Saviour. Immediately He was met with an outburst of violence as the demon sought to hush the voice of Christ as He explained the Scriptures to them. This is referred to again in Luke 4:33. After Christ has presented Himself as the One who fulfilled Isaiah's prophecy, we read, "In the synagogue there was a man, which had a spirit of an unclean demon, and cried out with a loud voice, Saying, Let us alone; what have we to do with thee, thou Jesus of Nazareth? art thou come to destroy us? I know thee who thou art: the Holy One of God." These were men indwelt by demons, and the demons used them to oppose Christ, to still the voice of Christ and to prevent Him from being received by the nation Israel.

Demons do not have the power to materialize themselves. They cannot assume a form or shape so that they can manifest themselves to men. They are dwellers in the unseen world, spirit beings who do not have a body of flesh and blood. To manifest their presence among men, demons must possess or control a physical body whether it be the body of an animal or the body of a man. We would not know of the presence of demons apart from the disorder that they produce when they control a man. It was evident to those in the synagogue in Capernaum that demons were present actively opposing Christ. The evidence was seen in the outburst that came through the lips of this demon-possessed man. There would have been no consciousness of demonic activity or demonic presence apart from the disorder in the synagogue. We find a good illustration of this fact in the 9th chapter of Luke's gospel. In verses 38 and 39 a man came to Christ, saying: "look upon my son: for he is mine only child. And, lo, a spirit [or demon] taketh him, and he suddenly crieth out; and it teareth him that he foameth again, and bruising him hardly departeth from him." It was evident to the father that a demon was possessing and controlling his son. The proof of that fact was in the disorganization and disarray, the confusion, the suffering, that was produced in the life of his only child.

Now the demons as they influenced men had their effect in several different areas. First of all we find that demons working in the physical realm could produce physical disease. Look in Matthew 9:32 and 33, "As they went out, behold, they brought to him a dumb man possessed with a demon. And when the demon was cast out, the dumb spake: and the multitudes marveled, saying, It was never so seen in Israel." Now the deafness, the dumbness, the physical infirmity that was produced by the demon was a very real sickness. It has to be treated as such. But there was a difference between being controlled by the demon and the physical sickness that resulted from demonic control, and Christ had to deal with both. He had to deliver the man from control by a demon and then deal with the physical effects of this demon's presence in his life. From many different illustrations in the gospels it can be substantiated that the demons could produce physical effects.

Demons affected men in the mental realm. In Matthew 17:15 a man came to Christ and said: "Lord have mercy on my son: for he is lunatic." This had to do with a mental derangement or a mental disorder and the presence of this demon robbed the son of his rational faculties so that his thought process was controlled not by the individual but by the demon.

We find that demons had influence in the emotional realm as well as the mental. This is inferred in Matthew 17:15 where the father said, "my son is sore vexed." In Mark 9:18 it is suggested to have been an effect in the emotional realm. A good illustration that Christ should heal this one for he "pineth away." This seems of this is the familiar record given to us in Luke 8:26-39. The demon-possessed individual we know as the Gadarene demoniac had been ostracized from his own community. He found his dwelling among the tombs. There he sat cutting himself. He was bound, hand and foot, as men sought to restrain him. Here is a vivid picture of what a demon could do. It affected his body so that he had to leave his place of residence. It affected his emotions for without doubt he sought out the tombs, an unclean place, because he felt unclean. He had a guilt complex. The man was cutting himself. This was because he was in such a mental state of depression that he counted himself unworthy to live, and that emotional state was produced by demoniac control. There the man sat utterly helpless and hopeless, brought to this situation, not by something that he had done, but because demons had used him to promote the purpose and program of Satan. We find then that the demons in the physical realm could produce physical sickness; in the mental realm they could produce insanity; in the emotional realm they could produce such depression that a man would seek to take his own life.

In a former pastorate I had a medical doctor in the congregation who was giving several days a week to serve in a state mental institution just a few miles from where we lived. On countless occasions this doctor said that the patient's need was not medicine but my ministry. It was the doctor's way of saying that the state of that individual was not attributable to physical causes but to spiritual causes or demoniac activity. This is something to which we have largely closed our minds, and we have denied that in so-called Christian America, Satan could have any influence upon individuals twenty centuries after the time of Christ. Satan's demonic activity is prevalent, real, and it is a part of our warfare about which we must be informed if we are to have victory over the Evil One.

Demons can control an unsaved man at will. The unsaved is a member of Satan's kingdom and submits to his authority and submits without resistance to control by demonic influence or activity. A believer can be controlled by Satan through demons only by the consent of his own will. Since the believer is a child of God and is in subjection to the authority of Christ, Christ will prevent that one from being indwelt by a demon. But demons may control a believer if the believer consciously submits to that control and influence. Since we have not recognized this possibility many believers may go through some physical affliction, some emotional disturbance or difficulty, some mental difficulty because they have not recognized the true source of the difficulty and come to deal with it on the principles of the Word of God.

There is a danger in speaking of these things, for it is possible to become so obsessed with demonic activity that it takes over one's thinking. I was sitting at breakfast with a friend in a restaurant. In the middle of our conversation he asked to be excused and he bowed his head and had a short prayer. We resumed our conversation. A few minutes later it happened again. I guess I looked somewhat quizzical and he explained that he was undergoing a satanic attack and he had to call upon Christ for deliverance. I said, "What makes you think that you are under satanic attack here?" He said, "Didn't you see that drop of coffee drop off the bottom of my coffee cup on my tie? That is a satanic attack." The second time he had let a little scrambled egg roll off the edge of his fork down into his lap and saw that as a satanic attack. I am not to say whether it was, or whether it wasn't. Maybe he had more spiritual discernment than I, but there is a danger that we become so obsessed with this adversary that we see him where he just doesn't exist. But that is not the great danger. The great danger is that we do not recognize his activity in our lives.

The Word of God gives us our defense against the attacks of the evil one. We have already referred to the account in Luke 4:35 where when Christ was confronted by the demon-possessed man in the synagogue He said, "Hold thy peace and come out of him." The authority of Christ was such that He could control demons. They did His will, and the demon left an habitation that he had been using to fulfill his purposes on the basis of the authority of Christ. In the 17th chapter of Matthew's gospel, while Christ was on the mount of transfiguration, the disciples were confronted by the father with the demon-possessed son, and they were not able to cast the demons out. When Christ returned and cast out the demon, the disciples wanted to know why they were impotent. Christ said, "Because of your unbelief: for verily I say unto you, If you have faith as a grain of mustard seed, ye shall say unto this mountain, Remove hence to yonder place; and it shall remove and nothing shall be impossible unto you. This kind goeth not out but by prayer and fasting." A mountain is used frequently in Scripture as the symbol of a kingdom and we believe it is so used here. What Christ was saying was this: If you have faith as a grain of mustard seed you shall say to this representative of Satan's kingdom, "Leave," and in response to your faith on the basis of the authority of Christ this representative of Satan's kingdom will flee. But this will not happen apart from prayer and fasting. Prayer and fasting were two evidences of complete dependence upon God. That is what prayer is: depending on God. And so Christ said that if we recognize that we have His authority, and believe that He makes us His partner in this warfare against Satan, and exercise His authority dependent upon God, we can say to any representative of Satan's kingdom, "You leave," and he will depart.

In Matthew 16:17 we find Christ said to Simon, "Simon Barjona; flesh and blood hath not revealed it unto thee, but my Father which is in heaven." Now the fact that had been revealed to Peter was the fact of the authority of Christ. He was the One who was to rule. And in His rule He would rule over, not only this world, but over the demonic realm as well. Christ says in Mark 16:16, "These signs shall follow them that believe; In my name shall they cast out demons." "In my name" does not mean some mysterious incantation, some magic formula that uses the name of Jesus. To speak in the name of a person is to use all his authority. Christ said that if we proceed against our adversary, or his representative, with His authority, dependent upon God, we can say to Satan, "Let me alone," and he will leave us alone.

Much that we suffer in the physical realm, the emotional realm and the mental realm we suffer because we are subject to Satan's attacks against us as an ambassador of Christ. We have not recognized that Satan is seeking to defeat the purpose of God in and through us. We let him continue to oppress us, to bring us into bondage through some physical, mental or emotional weakness. We have not by the authority of Christ resisted the devil that he might flee from us. We need to heed James's command, "Resist the devil," and claim His promise, "and he will flee from you" (James 4:7).

16

Christ's Conquest of Satan

Colossians 2:9 - 17

If you were to receive word from your doctor that you had been stricken with a fatal disease for which there was no known cure and as you shared this with me, I told you I had a certain cure, you would welcome that as good news indeed. I have better news for you than that. For while not all fall prey to one of the dread diseases, all were born into this world under the condemnation of sin. Sin stands between every individual and God, for He is holy and righteous and cannot receive an unholy thing into His presence. The good news is that found in Colossians 2:13, "God has forgiven you all trespasses."

The barrier of sin that once separated the sinner from God has been removed. The gulf of sin has been bridged. The condemnation lodged against the sinner has been removed. The death that characterized the sinner has been taken away, and the sinner has been made alive. That is the good news of the Gospel of Jesus Christ. Only eternity itself can reveal to us what it cost God to make such a simple offer of salvation to man. While the terms of the Gospel are simplicity itself, that which made this offer possible is as complex as the problem involved in satisfying a holy God.

The Apostle follows his great declaration that "God has forgiven you of all trespasses" by saying, "Blotting out the handwriting of ordinances that was against us, which was contrary to us, and took it out of the way, nailing it to his cross; and having spoiled principalities and powers, he made a shew of them openly, triumphing over them in it." Before God could declare salvation to sinners, it was necessary for Jesus Christ to enter into a conflict with Satan, to do battle with him, to come out of that battle as the victor, and to declare that Satan was a vanquished foe.

The Apostle Paul was familiar with Roman law. Under a very strict legal procedure, an accusing witness was interrogated by Roman authorities and his testimony substantiated before his case could be brought before the Roman court. When the indictment had been handed down and the case came to trial, it was necessary for the accuser to stand in the presence of the accused to give his testimony before the judge. It is that legal picture that Paul has in mind when he says that Christ has blotted out the handwriting of ordinances that was against us, contrary to us. In this instance the accuser is none other than Satan himself. Satan knows that God has declared that the soul that sins shall die. Satan knows that God has said that the wages of sin is death. He is reluctant to release control over any individual who is born into his kingdom. When Satan comes before God as an accuser, he points out before Him the sins of which man is guilty. Satan's accusation is just. It is fair and true, for there is no one apart from the Lord Jesus Christ born into this world who ever lived without sin. Paul had said in Romans 3:10, "There is none righteous, no, not one." And in verse 23, "For all have sinned, and come short of the glory of God." Satan does not have to look very far to find a catalog of crimes that he can use as a basis for accusation.

The Apostle says that God has blotted out the handwriting of ordinances that was against us. In other words, before God could forgive us all trespasses it was necessary to make a just disposition of the indictment that had been lodged against us. God recognized the fact that we were sinners. God did not pass over the fact that we were born in sin, that we practiced sin, and that we were under the condemnation of sin. God recognized it even before Satan accused us of crime. But before God could accept us into His family, before God could declare that we were forgiven our sins, it was necessary for Jesus Christ to do something about Satan's indictment. A just judge cannot hear an indictment and dismiss it if the indictment is true. Only if the indictment is false can the case be dismissed.

You will remember that when the Pharisees sought to put Christ to death they brought Him before the Roman authorities and accused Him of treason. The first step in Christ's trial was to examine Him concerning the indictment. Pilate withdrew Christ from the angry multitude and took Him within the judgment hall for questioning. He was acting as an investigator to see if the indictment lodged against Christ was true. He asked Christ concerning His kingdom and concerning His disciples, to discover how far this movement had spread, what Christ's attitude to Rome was, and whether He planned to overthrow Caesar. As Pilate interrogated Christ he readily recognized that no just indictment that could stand up in court had been lodged against Him. Thus he came out to face that angry multitude to say in effect, "I find no cause of offense in Him. He is innocent of the indictment with which you have charged Him."

It was at this point that the mob rose up against Pilate and screamed for Christ's blood and said they would accuse Pilate before the Roman Senate if he did not do as they wished. When Pilate, who was already being investigated by Rome, heard that they would add accusations against him to those already lodged, he sought to wash his hands of the blood of Christ, declaring that He was being delivered on a false indictment that could not stand up in a Roman court. Yet he bowed to the will of the people. We refer to that incident to show you that the Roman law system said an indictment had to be investigated before the accused could be tried.

The Apostle points out in Colossians 2:14 that our indictment lodged before God by Satan stood up because Paul says this indictment was "contrary to us." That suggests that the indictment had been investigated by the legal authorities and the indictment was found to be a true indictment. When Satan stood before God and pointed an accusing finger at you, we had already given ample proof of the fact that we were sinners and not acceptable in the presence of God. God could not honestly dismiss the case, because we were guilty. He could not let that indictment stand and accept us into glory as sinners, for we would defile the court of heaven.

Jesus Christ came to do something about the indictment. When a man stood guilty before the Roman tribunal of law there was only one just thing to do and that was to carry out the penalty that had been affixed for that transgression. In order for Jesus Christ to deal with the problem of the indictment that Satan made against us, it was necessary for Jesus Christ to die in our place. So the Apostle says that Christ removed the indictment by nailing it to His cross.

When any criminal was convicted and sentenced for a crime, an official writing was drawn up by the courts that explained the nature of the crime and its penalty. If the man were put into prison, that indictment was nailed to the prison door. When a man was guilty of some capital crime, an official indictment had to be written out and affixed to the cross. When Pilate delivered Jesus to be crucified he drew up the official Roman indictment and he wrote it out in three languages so that there would be no missing the accusation. The indictment was: "This is Jesus of Nazareth, the King of the Jews." That was to say, This man hangs here to die because He was found guilty of the crime of treason.

When Jesus Christ died, there was another indictment nailed to that cross, one not affixed there by a Roman nail. That indictment was put on the cross by Almighty God Himself. It was the list of your sins and mine. For when Jesus Christ went to the cross God placed on Him your iniquity and mine. All that God could charge us with was put on that cross so that when the angels of glory paraded past the cross of Jesus Christ there on Golgotha's hill they could read the list of your crimes and mine that put Jesus Christ on the cross. God did not forget one of them. Jesus Christ went to the cross carrying your indictment — everything for which you could be accused before God by Satan and all that would require God to dismiss you forever from His presence.

The Apostle says in Hebrews 2:14: "Forasmuch then as the

children are partakers of flesh and blood, Jesus Christ also himself likewise took part of the same: that through death he might destroy him that had the power of death, that is, the devil: And deliver them who through fear of death were all their lifetime subject to bondage." The Apostle is emphasizing that to provide forgiveness for you from *all* your sins, it was necessary for Jesus Christ to pay your debt to God, to take the indictment that Satan had lodged against you and satisfy it completely. Since the penalty for your sin and my sin is death, Jesus Christ had to die. Jesus Christ by His life could not pay the penalty for your sins and mine because the penalty for sin was not life; it was death. The debt was paid in full when Jesus Christ went to the cross bearing all of our sins, assuming our guilt, taking our indictment. The next time you look upon the form of a cross, recognize that God put your sins on Jesus' cross. God publicly displayed the indictment that sent the Son of God to die.

The second thing that the Apostle points out in Colossians 2:15 is that to forgive you all trespasses it was necessary, not only for Christ to die for your indictment, but for Him to triumph over the one who had lodged the indictment against you. This is what Paul says Christ did, "having spoiled principalities and powers, he made a show of them openly, triumphing over them in it." *Principalities* and *powers* is often used in Scripture for the entire hierarchy of demons under the authority of Satan (Ephesians 6:12). To provide salvation for men Jesus Christ had to win a victory over the accuser of men, that is, Satan himself.

According to Hebrews 2:14 the one who sought to destroy men and keep them in the power of death was the devil. The only way Jesus Christ could give us victory over Satan was to die for men and then to be brought to life again. Satan can destroy life. He cannot create life. Satan could bring about physical death but Satan could not bring a man to resurrection. So the Apostle who referred to the death of Christ in verse 14 refers to the resurrection of Christ in Colossians 2:15 to show us that the resurrection of Christ is God's victory over the accuser. Satan can never come before God and indict you for a sin again, because Jesus Christ has removed the indictment and because that debt has already been paid.

The Apostle writing in I Corinthians 15:3 summarizes the Gospel. It has two great facts included within it. First, Christ died for our sins according to the Scriptures. The proof that He died is attested there: He was buried. The second great fact of the Gospel is that Christ rose from the dead, and the proof is added: He was seen of many witnesses. The death of Christ and the resurrection of Christ are the two great facts upon which our salvation rests.

Before Paul leaves this great truth in Colossians 2:15 he says that, "Christ made a show of them openly, triumphing over them in it." Again Paul is referring to the custom in the Roman court. As we have already mentioned, a criminal's indictment was attached to the door of his cell so anyone passing by could know what he had been accused of and the penalty assessed. When a man had served his sentence and was released from prison, that indictment was taken down from the door, and the judge who had put him in prison would sign that indictment — he would write across it the word, *tetelestai*, which meant discharged or, "Paid in full." An individual who had served his time would take that cancelled indictment and nail it to his own front door. If questioned as to why he was out of jail, he could point to that indictment across which the judge had written *tetelestai*. He could rest in safety and security because the word *tetelestai* guaranteed his deliverance and his liberty.

When Jesus Christ hung on the cross just before He dismissed His spirit He said to the Father, "It is finished." The word translated "finished" is the word, *tetelestai*. What was He saying? Knowing that your sins and mine were nailed to that cross in that indictment which God had written, Jesus Christ with His own blood cancelled that indictment and wrote across it the same word that the court wrote across a cancelled indictment, *tetelestai*. God has the indictment lodged against you. The wages of sin is death but Jesus Christ went to the cross and paid that indictment. It is finished. It has been paid in full. Now God offers you a cancelled indictment. However, if you refuse to accept Jesus Christ as your own personal Saviour, it is as though Christ never died, and Satan's indictment against you still stands.

What have you done with that cancelled indictment that God offers you? Have you received it? Have you nailed it to your door? Do you rest in its safety, in its security? Or have you spurned that payment which Christ has made so that your debt still stands? To know Christ is to experience the forgiveness of sins, to be given eternal life. To reject Christ is to undergo the accusation of Satan forever and ever. God will forgive any sin but the sin of rejecting Jesus Christ as the Saviour who has paid your debt.

17

The Believer's Authority
Over Satan

Ephesians 2:1 - 10

It is quite common to hear Satan referred to as His Majesty, the Devil. But if we so refer to him, we are ascribing to him an authority which is not rightly his, for any authority that Satan has was usurped from God. Should a child of God attribute authority to Satan, he certainly will submit to the authority that he recognizes and will be brought under Satan's sway. We have been developing the biblical teaching concerning our adversary, something of his methods and his purposes. If we are to defeat our adversary it is also necessary for us to recognize the authority God has given us over Satan because we are related to Jesus Christ.

The Word of God makes it clear that Jesus Christ is the Creator of all things. It begins with a simple statement, "In the beginning, God created the heavens and the earth." As Scripture unfolds, it continually attributes the creative work to the Son of God. In Colossians 1:16, Paul very clearly asserts, "For by him [that is by Jesus Christ] were all things created, that are in heaven, and that are in earth, visible and invisible, whether they be thrones, or dominions, or principalities, or powers; all things were created by him, and for him." And when the Apostle refers to thrones, dominions, principalities and powers, he is referring to the hierarchies of created angelic beings referred to so frequently in the Word of God. These angelic beings were created by God. In John 1, the Apostle asserts that "All things were made by him, and without him is not anything made that was made." Jesus Christ is the Creator, not only of this material universe, but of the angelic realm as well.

Lucifer was one of God's created beings, and he, as it is recorded in Isaiah 14 and Ezekiel 28, rebelled against the Creator. He withheld the submission that was required of him as a created being. He declared himself to be independent of God, and he led an innumerable company of angels in his revolt against God. These angels who followed him became the demons who opposed the ministry of Christ during Christ's earthly sojourn.

We find in the gospels that Christ was in almost continuous conflict with demons. These demons were spirit beings; they possessed personality. Acknowledging Satan as their ruler they resisted God, God's program, and they opposed Jesus Christ. It is not without significance that many of Christ's miracles were performed in the demonic realm. He delivered men from bondage to Satan, from the physical infirmities and afflictions that were the result of Satan's control, or demonic control of the individuals. At the outset of His ministry, it was stated that Jesus Christ healed and cast out demons.

This is significant because Jesus Christ came not only to redeem, He came to reign. He came not only to be Saviour but to be sovereign. He came that He might wrest from Satan the scepter which Satan had taken from Adam, and that He might institute a kingdom on this earth. And if Jesus Christ is to reign on this earth as King of kings and Lord of lords, He must be able to subdue the usurper. Every miracle in the demonic realm was an attestation of Christ's authority over Satan. It was a demonstration of Christ's right to rule.

When Christ confronted the demons, they acknowledged His authority without any question. The Apostle James (James 2:19) asserts that the demons believed and trembled; or, as it would better be translated, the demons believed and shuddered. While men may give way to unbelief and skepticism concerning the person of Christ, no demon from hell has ever yet questioned the absolute deity of Jesus Christ. No demon has denied Christ's right to rule as King and His right to judge. And the demons anticipate a judgment yet to come. That is why James says the demons believe and shudder. They anticipate the manifestation of the authority of Jesus Christ.

When we turn to the gospels, we can select several examples of demons' submission to the authority of Christ, and their recognition of His absolute right to rule.

In the fifth chapter of Mark's gospel is recorded Christ's confrontation with a demon-possessed man whom we refer to as the maniac of Gadara. Beginning in the ninth verse, Christ asked the demon occupying this mad man, "What is thy name? And he answered, saying, My name is legion, for we are many. And he besought him much that he would not send them away out of the country. Now there was there nigh unto the mountains a great herd of swine feeding. And all the demons besought him, saying, Send us into the swine that we may enter into them. And forthwith Jesus gave them leave. And the unclean spirits went out, and entered into the swine; and the herd ran violently down a steep place into the sea, (they were about two thousand;) and were choked in the sea." Sufficient demons to occupy and to indwell a herd of 2,000 swine occupied the body of this one man! But as we read this record, we note that the demons could not make a move without permission from Christ, and when Christ gave a command, they responded immediately to the authority of Jesus Christ. They recognized His authority and were submissive to it.

In Mark 1:23, 24 we have another instance of this same thing. As Christ came into the synagogue in Capernaum, ". . . there was in their synagogue a man with an unclean spirit; and he cried out, saying, Let us alone, what have we to do with thee, thou Jesus of Nazareth? art thou come to destroy us? I know thee, who thou art, the Holy One of God." Notice that when Christ stood in the presence of this demon-possessed man, the demons recognized first of all the person of Christ. They acknowledged that He was the Holy One of God. They also recognized the right of Jesus Christ to judge demons for they asked Him, "Art thou come to destroy us?" Continuing in the 25th verse, "Jesus rebuked him, saying, hold thy peace, and come out of him. And when the unclean spirit had torn him, and cried with a loud voice, he came out of him." The demon resisted leaving the body that he had been occupying. He fought against submission to Christ by tearing at the man, but he was not able to resist the authority of Christ. These are only several of many instances that could be presented to you from the gospels to show that Christ had absolute authority in the Satanic realm.

In Colossians 2:15, Paul makes a statement to which we have referred before but which is of utmost importance in this consideration. Jesus Christ on the cross spoiled or robbed principalities and powers of their assumed authority, and He made a show of them openly, triumphing over them in it. Up to the time of the cross of Christ, Satan had claimed absolute authority in this earthly realm. He had set himself up as the prince of the powers of the air, as the god of this world, and he had claimed absolute authority. Jesus Christ in delivering man from demonic control during His earthly life had challenged Satan's authority. But it was not until Jesus Christ went to the cross that He joined battle about this question of authority, and by His death and resurrection demonstrated incontrovertibly His absolute authority over Satan. The cross of Christ is God's answer concerning the authority of His Son. The death and resurrection of Christ reveal that Satan is a usurper. The cross of Christ stands, then, as God's basis of deliverance from Satanic power.

As we carry this a step further, we find that, after the death and resurrection of Christ, the absolute authority of Christ was established by the Father. In Philippians 2:9-11, Paul writes: "God also hath highly exalted him [that is the Son] and given him a name which is above every name; that at the name of Jesus every knee should bow, of things in heaven, and things in earth, and things under the earth; and that every tongue should confess that Jesus Christ is Lord to the glory of God the Father." There has been question concerning the three realms of authority mentioned in verse 10. It seems that the things in heaven refer to the sphere of God; things in earth refer to this natural realm, the human sphere; things under the earth refer to the Satanic sphere or the demonic realm. In these three spheres there is only one individual who is recognized as Lord, One who has absolute authority, and that is Jesus Christ. Satan does not have absolute authority; Jesus Christ is Lord and beside Him there is no other. This same truth is given to us in Ephesians 1:19-22 where Paul prays "that they might know what is the exceeding greatness of his power to usward who believe, according to the working of his mighty power, which he wrought in Christ, when he raised him from the dead and set him at his own right hand in heavenly places [now notice], far above all principality, and power, and might, and dominion, and every name that is named, not only in this world but also in that which is to come; and hath put all things under his feet. . . . " Now Paul is affirming there what we saw stated in Philippians 2, that, at the resurrection of Christ, God demonstrated that all authority belongs to His Son, and that all others who claim to have authority are making a false claim.

Jesus Christ, when He came into the world, challenged Satan. He challenged Satan's right to be worshiped; He challenged Satan's right to be believed; He challenged Satan's control. When Jesus Christ went to the cross, He entered into combat with Satan and, by defeating Satan through the resurrection, He authenticated His authority. And God, by receiving Him up into glory, demonstrated that He was enthroning Jesus Christ in the place of authority and that men were obligated to obey Him, to believe Him, to trust Him, and no other.

When we continue into the second chapter of Ephesians, we find the authority of Christ now belongs to the believer *because* the believer is associated with Jesus Christ. We, of ourselves, have no authority over Satan. The Psalmist tells us in Psalm 8 that in God's order of creation angels are on a level above men. Men were created a little lower than the angels if you were to stratify God's creation. God as Creator, the uncreated one, is of course the apex. Under God were the angelic beings, then lower than the angels the human race. Then under the human race, animal creation. Below that the vegetable creation. Man does not and cannot have authority over the angels, because man was not put in superiority over angels at the time of his creation. The point, then, is that as a human being we can have no authority over an angel, nor can we have authority over fallen angels, over demons or over Satan. By creation we are a lesser grade of created being than angels. If man is to have authority over Satan and the Satanic realm, he must be given an authority that is greater than man's authority invested by creation.

This is important because, until we realize that we have no authority of ourselves or as human beings, we will live a continuously defeated life, subject to the authority of Satan because we have not appropriated that which has been given to us by Jesus Christ. Christ by His resurrection was placed in authority over every realm. May we remind you again what Paul says in Ephesians 1:20: "Which he wrought in Christ, when he raised him from the dead, and set him at his own right hand in heavenly places, far above all principality and power, and might, and dominion, and every name that is named. . . . and hath put all things under his feet. . . . [1:22]: And you. . . . [2:1]" Underline the two first words in Ephesians 2. He raised him and set him at his own right hand . . . *and you.* Jesus Christ has joined us to Himself so that we were identified with Him. By the work of the Holy Spirit, when Jesus Christ died, we died. When Jesus Christ was buried, we were buried. When Jesus Christ was resurrected, we were resurrected. When Jesus Christ ascended and was seated at the right hand of the father, we ascended and were seated with Him. Christ and the believer can never be separated. We participated in all that Jesus Christ has done. He has joined us to Himself so that the Apostle can say, "God raised him . . . and you." God set Him at His own right hand . . . and you. And has put all things under His feet and under yours, because (verse 5), "Even when we were dead in sins, hath quickened us [or made us alive] together with Christ, and has raised us up together, and has made us sit together in heavenly places in Christ Jesus."

What is Paul teaching? That when Christ arose, we believers arose with Him. When Christ ascended, we believers ascended with Him. When Christ was seated at the Father's right hand, we believers were seated with Jesus Christ. And when God gave the Son authority over the angelic realm and over the realm of Satan, He gave us that authority *because* we are in Christ Jesus. Now the believer has an authority over Satan that he did not have as a natural man. He was under the angels by the fact of his creation, but by virtue of his new creation in Jesus Christ he is elevated to a position above angels. He is seated with Christ in the heavenlies, and he has the authority that belongs to Jesus Christ conferred upon him by God the Father.

The believer, then, has been given the authority of Christ over Satan. But as long as you refer to your adversary as "his majesty, the devil," you are going to be taking orders from him, submitting to him, because you are attributing to him the authority that he claims to have but that Jesus Christ has demonstrated by His death to be an absolute fraud. You are being taken in by a deceiver. He is the greatest con artist this world has ever seen. He is deceiving many because they have convinced themselves they are helpless, that they can't resist him, and there is nothing they can do against him, and, when he pulls the string, they have to dance. That is a lie of the devil. As a believer, you have authority over Satan and over Satan's minions because you have been joined to Jesus Christ and have the same authority that Jesus Christ has. That is the grace of God given to us.

What authority did Christ have over Satan? In Matthew 16, Peter had no sooner spoken his words of confession, "Thou art the Christ the Son of the Living God," than Satan got busy. Why? The last thing that he wanted Peter to do was confess that Jesus Christ was Lord. After Peter made his confession of faith, Christ told the disciples He was going to Jerusalem to die. And in verse 22, "Peter took him, and began to rebuke him, saying, Be it far from thee, Lord: this shall not be unto thee." And the word translated "rebuke" is the word that literally means to take one by the shoulders and shake him. Peter was trying to shake some sense into the Lord Jesus Christ. Christ turned, and these are His words, "Get thee behind me, Satan, for thou art an offence unto me, for thou savorest not the things that be of God but those that be of men." Christ recognized that Peter was a vehicle being used by Satan to mouth his own philosophy. And Christ spoke to Satan directly and said, "Get thee behind me, Satan, thou art an offence to me." He repudiated what Satan had to say, and what he was trying to do.

What effect did this have? What did Peter learn from this?

Turn to I Peter 5:8. Peter got an education but the tuition cost was high. This is what he learned from that classroom experience. "Be sober, be vigilant; because your adversary the devil as a roaring lion, walketh about seeking whom he may devour; whom resist steadfast in the faith, knowing that the same afflictions are accomplished in your brethren that are in the world." Peter wanted his flock to remember that Satan is stalking their path every step they take. What are they to do? Run? They can't outrun him. Hide? They can't hide from him. Peter tells them in verse 9: "resist steadfast in the faith." Notice that word "resist." That word in the original text is a word that means *to stand against*. Now this is not a defensive word. It is an offensive word. It is important for us to observe this. When Satan puts some temptation in front of us, we think the best thing to do is to run, to flee from it. There are some things we are told to flee from, but we are never in Scripture told to run from the devil.

God's method of defeating the devil is not to try to outrun him. That can't be done. After all, when an angel can go from the east to the west in a moment of time because he is a spirit being, how do you think you can outrun him? You can't do it. He is there waiting for you when you come panting in at the end of your flight. No, God's method of meeting the devil is to launch a counter-offensive, to resist him, or to stand actively against him. Remember, that is what Christ did at His temptation. He wasn't out there running in the rocks trying to hide from Satan, with Satan inadvertently coming upon Him. No. Christ was out there forcing Satan to meet Him, to join the conflict. Now that is what Peter has learned. He saw Christ meet this temptation that came to Peter by actively resisting or standing against, or repudiating Satan. And Peter said to his sheep: "The only way you can withstand Satan, the only way you can meet Satan is to oppose him actively, steadfast in the faith."

Turn to James 4:7: "Submit yourselves therefore to God, resist the devil, and he will flee from you." Now there you have the same word again. It is translated "resist" as it was in I Peter 5:9, and it has the same sense: "actively oppose Satan and, when you do, he will flee from you." You see, since Satan is referred to as a roaring lion, we think that Satan has no fear. But we don't realize that Satan is an abject coward. We talk about the fearlessness of a lion. But, after a lion has made a kill, he roars to frighten away the jackals or the other animals that wait for someone else to do their killing and then rob what the lion has killed. So the roar of a lion after a kill arises because the lion is afraid of the jackals. The jackals will come and steal what he has gotten for himself. The roar of a lion is not an evidence of his fearlessness. It is an evidence of his cowardice. But Satan has you fooled. You think he is absolutely without fear and isn't afraid of you or anything you can do. He wants you to believe that. But James tells us that, if you actively oppose Satan, he will turn tail and run. This is the authority of the believer. The believer, because he is enthroned with Jesus Christ, can exercise the authority of Christ, and Satan can no more withstand the authority of Christ that you exercise than he can go against the authority of Jesus Christ that issues from the throne of God.

Consider now Ephesians 6:13: "Wherefore take unto you the whole armor of God, that ye may be able to withstand in the evil day, and having done all, to stand." The word "withstand" is exactly the same Greek word used in I Peter 5:9 or in James 4:7 and it means *to resist* or *to stand against*. This is launching the offensive. And what Paul says is that when you by faith appropriate the whole armor of God so that your person is protected, you can then launch your offensive. Because Satan is a coward he will flee when you resist him in the name of Jesus Christ, and with the authority of Christ you will be able to stand. There is no standing apart from an offensive, and there will be no victory apart from the exercise of the authority of Christ.

God has not saved us, made us His children, and brought us into His family that we should live a life of defeat. He has not brought us into His family that we should live in a cowering fear of our adversary as though he were absolutely irresistible and we were utterly helpless, and every time he pursued us we had to fall. The Word of God declares that Jesus Christ's victory and triumph over Satan is absolute. God has given Him all authority, and Jesus Christ has conferred upon us the same authority. Therefore, we may resist Satan as effectively as Jesus Christ resisted him when He looked at Peter and said, "Get thee behind me, Satan."

If you were to hear some friend whom you knew was being subjected to some Satanic temptation say, "Get thee behind me, Satan," you would probably be surprised. It shows how little we comprehend the plan of God for our victory over the evil one. Such a truth is clearly revealed in the Book, that God has conferred upon you as His child the same authority that belonged to Jesus Christ. And God expects you to be actually engaged in conflict, in warring against the adversary, in exercising the authority that God has given to you so that you are withstanding or resisting or standing against the attacks of the evil one. We have no rights of ourselves; we cannot wage a warfare apart from the enablement of the Holy Spirit. You need not cower, you need not cringe, and you need not try to run, for you can use the authority that there is in your position as a son of God. You can use the power that was released at the cross of Christ to stand against the evil one so that he will flee from you.

Many of us go through constant temptations and subject ourselves to incessant fears because we have never appropriated and exercised the authority that God has given to us. The next time you feel your steps dogged by Satan, exercise your faith in the promise of God and turn to that one who has been pursuing you and say, "I resist you on the authority of Christ and by the blood of Christ." Instead of listening to your own footsteps trying to outrun Satan, you will hear his footsteps as he runs from the authority that God has given to you. You are God's child. You have been enthroned. You have been given the authority of Christ, and God expects you to use it actively and resist, to withstand, to put to flight the evil one.

Would God lie? Would God send you to do battle with weapons that were not adequate? Of course not. So, if God tells you to withstand the evil one by the authority of Christ, "Resist the devil and he will flee from you."

18

Putting the Adversary to Flight

James 4:1 - 8

Recently I was given a 31 caliber bullet captured from a Viet-cong soldier. It was ingeniously engineered so that, when it strikes an object, it tumbles end over end and tears its way through bringing death and destruction in its wake. Yet, if this one were put into the rifle and pointed toward me and the trigger fired, I would not be the least bit afraid of it because the bullet has been deactivated. The powder has been removed and it has been rendered absolutely harmless. However, if you did not know that, and it were placed in a rifle and pointed at you, and you knew it was the intention of the one holding the rifle to fire it, you would run for the nearest cover and cower in dread and terror. But knowing that it had been safely deactivated, you would be completely unconcerned.

Many live in fear and fall in defeat before our adversary, the devil, because they do not realize the biblical principle that he has been deactivated and has been rendered harmless. And every time he appears, they cower before him and are overcome. They are convinced that they must go down in defeat because they have not appropriated the principle that Jesus Christ through His death has rendered Satan inoperative and has given us the means of victory. Let us develop a step further the promise given to us in James 4:7: "Resist the devil and he will flee from you."

The word "resist" does not call for passive resistance, does not suggest to us a futile attempt to defend ourselves. It pictures a soldier of Jesus Christ marching out to do combat with the adversary with the full and complete assurance that we have victory already given to us through the One who has led us in the train of His triumph. And when the Apostle instructs us: "Resist the devil," he is standing as a general before those troops under his authority and commanding, "Forward, march!" He is not calling retreat. He is not sounding an alarm to send God's soldiers into a foxhole because they have no defense against the adversary. The Apostle is commanding us to do battle with Satan because he has the assurance that, when he is actively opposed on the basis of scriptural principles, he will and must flee from before our attack.

In Peter's similar command (I Peter 5:9) he said in effect, "You turn and face him. You resist him. You actively oppose him, and through your active opposition, you will turn this one to flight. The pursuer will become the pursued." Especially notice one phrase that the Apostle has placed in this exhortation: "Resist *steadfast in the faith.*"

When he refers to the faith, he is not referring to the body of divine truth that is revealed to us in the Word of God. That is the faith once and for all delivered to the saints. He is saying "stand steadfast in the faith principle." Stand by faith. The Apostle is selecting out from the entire body of revealed truth one particular aspect of divine truth that applies to our conflict with the adversary. Now what truth does he have in mind which we are called on to believe?

The first truth is the truth of the authority of the believer. In the Epistle of Jude, we read in verses 8 and 9: "Likewise also these filthy dreamers defile the flesh, despite dominion, speak evil of dignities. Yet Michael the archangel, when contending with the devil he disputed about the body of Moses, durst not bring against him a railing accusation, but said, The Lord rebuke thee." Recall what we have emphasized previously — God has given to the believer in the Lord Jesus Christ an authority that exceeds the authority of our adversary. When Lucifer was created, he was created as the highest of the archangels of God. Now even though Lucifer rebelled and became Satan or the Devil, the rest of the angelic realm remembered and recognized the authority that he had had by creation. Michael was an archangel. According to the hierarchy arranged at the time of angelic creation, Michael would have been only one step below Lucifer, directly responsible to Lucifer, who in turn was responsible to God. Although Lucifer rebelled and became Satan, Michael never could forget that by creation Lucifer had been his superior.

Much later, after the fall of Satan, when Michael and Satan entered into conflict over the body of Moses, Michael did not dare to stand alone against Lucifer. In this conflict over the body of Moses, Michael, who now is vastly superior to Satan, because he is an unfallen angel, called upon God and said, "The Lord rebuke thee." Not even an unfallen angel dared try to exert authority over Satan. The unfallen angels trusted God to defeat Satan in the conflicts into which they had been sent by God. Michael was not in conflict with Satan by his own will, nor to pursue his own purposes. Michael was in that conflict over the body of Moses because God sent him on that mission. But the authority of Michael was not sufficient in itself to defeat Satan. He had to call upon God by faith.

The great truth of Ephesians 2 is that when Jesus Christ was resurrected and ascended and enthroned in glory, you and I as believers in Jesus Christ were enthroned with Him. God has raised Him from the dead, and you. God has brought Him into glory and brought you into glory with Him. Paul says in Ephesians 2:6: "God has raised us up together and has made us sit together in heavenly places in Christ Jesus." Because we are associated with Christ on the throne of God, the authority of the throne belongs to the child of God in our conflict with the evil one. We have an authority over Satan that exceeds the authority that Michael had. But as Michael did not dare enter into conflict with Satan alone but called upon God to give him victory, so we need to be reminded that we need and have God's authority, and this authority is to be exercised by faith.

How do we know this is true? The Word of God says so. This is something that must be believed. And the first step in victory over Satan is the step of faith, a step that believes God, a step that believes the Word of God. When Peter writes to his fearful sheep who were entering into conflict with a roaring lion, and exhorts them to stand "steadfast in the faith," he is saying to them that when they hear the adversary approaching, they are to believe what God says — that they have authority over him and can turn him back. If you believe that you are helpless before Satan, if you believe that you have no means to victory, if you are convinced that every time he speaks you must obey, if you believe that every time he tempts you you must fall, you will obey, you will be defeated, you will fall. But when you believe that you have been given authority over Satan, then you can actively resist him, and forbid him to pursue the course that would bring about your destruction or downfall.

The second thing we are called upon to believe if we are to be victorious over Satan is the fact that Satan is a defeated enemy. It is a strange thing as we go through the Word of God to find what universal agreement there is on this fact. Turn to Matthew 8:29, for instance. We find that all of the demons in hell acknowledge the fact of their defeat. We read there that when Christ came into the country of the Gergesenes, there met Him two coming out of the tombs, exceeding fierce, so that no man might pass by that way. And in verse 29 it is recorded, "[The demons] cried out saying, What have we to do with thee, Jesus, thou Son of God? Art thou come hither to torment us before the time?" The word *torment* has to do with consignment to eternal punishment, the eternal torment of the damned. These demons who stood face to face with Jesus Christ, recognized that He is their judge and they are condemned to be separated from God forever. They anticipated a coming judgment on fallen angels in which they will be banished from the presence of God eternally. Thus, when they faced Christ, they asked if He had come before they expected it. This verse shows us that the demons recognize that Satan has been defeated and, because they are his, they suffer defeat.

Not only the demons but Satan himself acknowledges that defeat. John writes in Revelation 12:12, "Therefore rejoice ye heavens, and ye that dwell in them. Woe to the inhabiters of the earth and the sea! for the devil is come down unto you, having great wrath, because he knoweth that he hath but a short

time." John, of course, is describing Satan's activity in the tribulation period. The frenzy of the last part of the tribulation period
John attributes to Satan's knowledge that the time when he will
be bound and cast into the Lake of Fire is fast approaching, that
what he does he must do immediately. Satan acknowledges the
fact of his defeat, the fact that he has been judged and is to be
confined to the Lake of Fire forever. Demons and Satan do not
argue the fact; they accept it and acknowledge it.

God in other passages states the fact of Satan's defeat. In
Colossians 2:15, Paul states that Christ by His death spoiled
principalities and powers, that is, robbed them of their authority.
He made a show of them openly, triumphing over them in it.
And again in II Corinthians 2:14, Paul writes, "Thanks be unto
God which always causeth us to triumph in Christ." We might
read that verse, "Thanks be to God which always leads us in the
train of Christ's triumph." The picture there is one of a victorious
general returning from a military conquest. In these passages in
which the Apostle pictures Christ as a victor, he is stating again
the truth that all heaven knows, that Jesus Christ by His death
and resurrection has triumphed over Satan, and will lead in
triumph all those who believe that they are victors. And when
Peter exhorts his sheep, pursued by a roaring lion, to stand
"steadfast in the faith," he wants them to hold on to the truth,
not only that they have been given God's authority over Satan,
but that they may parade as victors because Jesus Christ is the
Victor over the evil one.

We recognize that the resurrection of Jesus Christ is a keystone
of our faith. When Paul summarized the Gospel to the Corinthians, he stripped it down to its barest essentials and said we
have preached a Gospel that Christ died for our sins, and that
He rose again the third day. The death of Christ provides a
basis for our salvation through the shedding of blood. The resurrection of Christ not only signifies God's acceptance of Christ's
death as a payment for our sins, but the resurrection provides the
basis for the believer's daily victory over the adversary. And
while hell cannot forget that Christ rose as a victor and while all
heaven acknowledges the fact that Jesus Christ arose, we who

live here seem to live as though He were still bound in the grave. Jesus Christ came forth as a victor in order that we might walk in the train of His triumph, that we might fight a good warfare by faith in His victory.

There is a third truth that must be believed if we are to have victory over the evil one. Not only are we called upon to believe in the authority of the believer that exceeds the authority of angels, not only are we to believe that Satan has been defeated, but we are to believe the categorical promise of God, "Resist the devil and he will flee from you" (James 4:7). Actively oppose Satan on the basis of the truth that the Word of God reveals about him and he will flee. When blood was applied to the doorposts and the lintels of the homes in Egypt, the death angel could not enter. There was no force in hell that could pry open a door that had been sealed by blood. And when you are undergoing some Satanic attack — whether it be a temptation to sin, whether it be some oppression or depression in the realm of the mind, whether it be in the realm of the affections in which your love of Christ is being diverted away to other things — no matter what the forms of the attack, when you plead the value of the blood of Christ, Satan cannot pursue the attack. He can only turn and run because he hates the sight of blood. Your victory is based on the value of the death of Christ, a death that not only provides for salvation from the condemnation of sin, but a death that protects you from the onslaughts of the evil one.

As believers in Christ, we can also plead the benefits of the resurrection of Christ. We only need remind the adversary that a resurrected, glorified Christ is the captain of our salvation, that we take orders from Him. Satan turns from the battle because he is a coward and will not fight where there is no hope of victory. When the child of God pleads the value of the cross of Christ and pleads the victory and the triumph of a resurrected Christ, Satan's defeat is absolutely certain. The tragedy is that, when we have the means of victory in our hands, we turn from the faith principle and join in a hand-to-hand combat with Satan and then wonder why we go down to defeat. Can you imagine anything more foolish than sending our soldiers into battle with no weapons whatsoever? Yet that's the way many are trying to do battle with Satan. You have left every weapon behind and have thought by your own cunning, by your own skill, by your own deception, you could camouflage yourself and defeat the enemy. It has never been done yet. If you are to experience victory, you will realize it by faith, believing what God says about your position in Christ.

God has not called upon you to hide, called upon you to run, called upon you to outsmart the adversary. He has called upon you to cover yourself with the armor of God, then to withstand him actively, believing what the Word of God says about your authority and your victory, and to put the adversary to flight because you are joined with the Victor. May you, when you recognize the presence of the adversary, actively resist him because you believe what God has said about your invincibility, what God has said about your authority, what God has said about your victory.

19

Trafficking With Demons

Deuteronomy 18:9 - 11

Man has an insatiable curiosity about the future. Even though he is unable to cope with all the problems that the present brings, he still wants to assume the burden of the future. By one means or another he seeks to discover what lies ahead. This is not a new phenomenon; it is as old as the human race. As we go back into the earlier chapters of the Word of God we find that men there sought to find out concerning coming events.

God has seen fit to take us into confidence concerning some of His program. The Word of God is authenticated, if for no other reason, because it contains many prophecies which we can examine for understanding and edification. But when a man goes beyond what has been written in the Word of God he is subject to delusion; he is subject to deception through the activity of Satan through his demons.

Any contact with demons is expressly forbidden in the Word of God. This was so prevalent, even in Israel's experience in the Old Testament, that God had to give the commandment in Exodus 22:18, "Thou shalt not suffer a witch to live." There was evidently something very serious about witchcraft, for to practice witchcraft brought the witch under a death penalty. We have to be careful concerning our definition of a witch. Our thinking is molded a good deal by medieval theology and by the practices in colonial days in New England. Our concept of a witch is one who calls down a curse upon an individual. Such a concept says that a witch could bring physical, mental, or emotional harm to an individual upon whom a spell was cast. But the Word of God has no such concept of a witch. The word translated *witch* in the Old Testament means *one who knows, one who prognosticates, one who foretells the future.* Witchcraft in the Old Testament was a demonic means by which future events were revealed to an individual who submitted himself or herself to control by demons.

In its early experience, Israel was not satisfied with the revelation which God had given concerning His program. There were those who sought to know more about events. Not satisfied with the revelation that God gave in the Word, they consulted demons that they might receive revelation concerning the future. To discount the authority of the Word of God, to deny the sufficiency of the revelation of the Word of God, and to consort with demons to obtain further information which God had not seen fit to reveal brought such a one under a death sentence.

Witchcraft or sorcery is dealt with in the eighteenth chapter of the book of Deuteronomy. In verse 9 God said through Moses, "When thou art come into the land which the Lord thy God giveth thee, thou shalt not learn to do after the abominations of those nations." We know that the land of Canaan to which God brought the children of Israel after their redemption from Egypt was populated by many different tribes and peoples who had one thing in common: they worshiped demons and they had practices of consorting with demons in the religious realm under the guise of worship. These demons were worshiped by all sorts of abominable practices, by all sorts of perversions and immorality, even by human sacrifices. God was bringing the nation Israel, who had received an authoritative revelation from God, into the land where He knew they would be subject to influence by these heathen religions, and God warned them concerning these practices. Then in verses 10 and 11 the various forms of this activity in the name of religion are outlined: "There shall not be found among you anyone that maketh his son or his daughter to pass through the fire. . . . " That refers to the experience of offering children as human sacrifices to these deities of the Canaanites. Were you to go to Byblos today you would see the excavations of the ancient Canaanite worship, and the guide would point out to you the stone platforms where these sacrifices of children to their demonic deities were practiced. God forbade it.

Along with human sacrifice there were other things God forbade that were just as grievous to Him. God said, "There shall not be found among you . . . one that useth divination, or an observer of times, or an enchanter, or a witch, or a charmer, or a consulter with familiar spirits, or a wizard, or a necromancer. For all that do these things are an abomination unto the Lord." God speaks here of many different forms of contact or traffic with demons practiced in the land to which Israel was going. There were those who used divination, which was a process of foretelling the future by magical means. They usually practiced some form of augury, investigating the entrails of a bird or an animal to discover the future or determine a course of action. If you have read Roman history, you are familiar with the Roman Augurs who forecast and predicted the outcome of Roman military movements by sacrificing animals and then examining the entrails. This became the determinative movement in Roman military conquests. They depended upon this form of traffic with demons. God said that was forbidden.

Next, there was not to be found among them an observer of times. This has to do with determining or directing the course of an individual's life or determining his conduct by contact with the stars or studying astrology. I need not remind you of how common and widespread this practice is today. I saw a report recently of the unprecedented volume of mail that a local newspaper received when inadvertently the daily horoscope was omitted from the paper. People were unable to make any decisions during the day! God forbade the Israelites to "observe times" for that was a form of demonism.

The next thing that God referred to was the enchanter. The enchanter was one under demonic control who brought another individual under demonic control with his enchantments. This has to do with casting a spell and perhaps comes closer to our ordinary concept of a witch than any of these others.

Another form of traffic with demons forbidden was the witch. The word *witch* here refers to one who knows. Thus some individuals found it impossible to make any decision until they had consulted an astrologer or prognosticator.

Then there was the charmer. The charmer was one who used magic and worked miracles by demonic power. The wise men of Egypt had this kind of power in that they could imitate by demonic activity the miracles of God which Moses performed. Daniel encountered this same type of demonic activity in the courts of the King of Babylon. He was surrounded by the wise men of Babylon who, through their incantations and prognostications under demonic control, were able to direct the course of the empire as they guided Nebuchadnezzar. These charmers were another form of trafficking with evil spirits.

God refers next to the consulter with familiar spirits. This was the individual who was on personal terms with, and under control of, a demon. An individual could not be brought under control apart from voluntary submission. The demon did not have power to master and overrule the will of an individual so that he was possessed apart from his consent. Consulters voluntarily submitted themselves so that the spirits could reveal future things to them and they, in turn, could become contacts between an inquirer and demons. We refer to such consulters today as spirit mediums.

Next there was the wizard. The wizard is the masculine of witch. The wizard was the man who knew. This was not something which only the woman could practice.

The necromancer was one who gained his information from departed dead ones. A demon was a contact between the living world and the world of departed spirits to provide some knowledge of future things.

From Deuteronomy 18:10, 11 you see how widespread this practice was in Israel and how many different forms it took. The purpose of all these different forms of demonism was to gain information apart from the Word of God to guide men in their actions or decisions. We perhaps are tempted to think that this is something that was practiced only in a superstitious age. But as we go through the Word of God we find that it was as prevalent in New Testament times as it was in the Old Testament.

And in vast areas of the earth today it is the dominant form of religious experience or practice among those who do not know Jesus Christ as a personal Saviour.

Consider the illustration of this type of trafficking with demons in the experience of Saul as it is recorded in I Samuel 28:1-6. To many, this has been a puzzling passage of Scripture. Notice, first of all, the background of this experience. Saul, the king in Israel, was being attacked by the Philistines, his strongest adversaries. Saul depended upon Samuel, the prophet of the Lord, for guidance and counsel. Samuel had died, and Saul felt that he had no source of guidance in this national crisis. Now Saul did have the Scriptures that had been given by God through Moses and they were sufficient to guide Saul in his course of conduct. But because he repudiated the revelation which God gave in His Word, Saul sought some other guidance. He commanded in verse 7, "Seek me a woman that hath a familiar spirit, that I may go to her, and enquire of her." He wanted a woman who was on familiar terms with some demon so that he could gain knowledge by contacting one who was dead. Notice that the Scripture does not say that such a practice is impossible. It says that such a practice is forbidden, but it did not say it was impossible. Saul knew that the Word of God forbade such activity because in verse 3 we read that Saul had put away those that had familiar spirits and the wizards out of the land. In spite of what he knew, Saul sought out this woman of Endor. She is not called a witch. The word literally translated means she is the mistress of the demon. After Saul had granted her immunity from punishment, she said, "Whom shall I bring up unto thee? and he said, Bring me up Samuel." Now why would Saul want to contact the godly prophet Samuel? Obviously it was that he might learn from this prophet what God had for him in the future. "And when the woman saw Samuel she cried with a loud voice." This reaction suggests to us that the woman who had the familiar spirit was absolutely dumbfounded when Samuel materialized. She expected the familiar spirit to appear and then through the familiar spirit she hoped to make contact with Samuel. When Samuel appeared she was amazed because she had no contact with

Samuel and he was not her familiar spirit. Saul inquired of her "what form he is of?" When she described the one who appeared to her, Saul said that it must be Samuel. Note that Saul did not see Samuel. The woman saw Samuel, but Saul did not. Saul could not have contact with one who had departed except through a demon and he was not under control of a demon. Samuel appeared, not because he was summoned by demons, but because he was sent by God to announce judgment upon Saul and announce the overthrow of Saul's kingdom. This certainly does not set a pattern, but it does show that one who had submitted herself to a demon could gain information concerning future things through demonic activity.

In Acts 8:9 we find that the same practice was carried on in New Testament times. Philip, the evangelist was ministering in Samaria. He preached Christ and proclaimed Him as the Saviour from sin, the Deliverer from Satan. There was in that city a man called Simon, who had used sorcery. He had contact with a demon to perform magical works and to reveal future events. He had bewitched the people of Samaria; that is, he had impressed them with his knowledge of the future which he had gained through demonic means, and as a result of his contact with demons he was credited with having power from God. People said of Simon (v. 10), "This man is the great power of God." They were not able to distinguish between the magic performed by demonic power and miracles performed by divine power. It is Satan's purpose to get men to believe that he is God and to give him the worship that belongs to God. We are reminded that Satan's original desire was to be like the most High, to receive the worship that belongs to God. God demonstrates that He is God by the miracles that He performs, and by the future that He reveals through prophecy. It is significant that when Satan seeks to authenticate himself he does it by causing those who are under control of his demons to work miracles and to reveal the future. We find this in the case of Simon. Such was the subtlety of Satan who controlled this man so as to convince the people in Samaria that he was God.

The only deliverance from this demonic influence was the

Gospel of Jesus Christ. We read in Acts 8:12, "When they believed Philip . . . they were baptized, both men and women, then Simon himself believed also, and when he was baptized, he continued with Philip, and wondered, beholding the miracles and signs which were done." The people of Samaria who had listened to Simon were delivered from demonic influence by believing the Gospel of Jesus Christ, and the sorcerer himself was delivered from demonic influence and control the same way. The Gospel was authenticated by the miracles which the Apostles produced. So God used Philip to give an evidence to these who had trafficked with demons that He was God and Satan was an imposter.

Satan's program has worked well from the time of the Old Testament down to the present day. Men have been deluded as Satan has worked through these different forms of demonism to keep men's minds darkened to the truth. Many have been convinced that because Satan's demons can reveal future events or contact the dead that he is actually God. We are told in the Word of God that the closer we come to the end time, the greater Satan's activity will be. John tells us in Revelation 12:12 that Satan knowing that his time is short goeth forth furiously to deceive and to destroy. We have been so little apprised of Satan's method and his working through demonic activity we have not been prepared to meet him.

Only a short time ago a very widely-read book appeared in which the author claims to be able to predict future events. She made a number of predictions that did come true. These predictions can come only from one of two possible sources: either from God, or from Satan through demonic influence. God has made it very clear that with the completion of the New Testament, He is not making further revelations and predictions. God has closed the door to new revelations from God because revelation is completed in Jesus Christ. That leaves only one alternative. These predictions must come through demonic influence from Satan. Certain of these predictions have been sufficiently startling to deceive even many believers that she must come with divine authority. She and others like her have become advisors of some people high in government. This is demonic activity! It controls nations, it influences governments to substitute for the authority and the Word of God the revelations that come from demons.

Other forms of demonic activity prevail. They include astrology, horoscopes, and influence of stars upon daily life. E. S. P. (extrasensory perception) is considered by many as a phenomenon of the natural mind. They attribute to the mind of men those qualities that belong only to God, and fail to see demonic influence and activity in this realm. It is another way by which Satan seeks to control the minds of men. Many have experimented with a Ouija board. What a harmless and innocuous thing a Ouija board is. With just a little practice you could manipulate and get the answers that you want. When so used it is a perfectly harmless thing, but when one surrenders the control of his faculties and submits to influence outside of himself he is rendering himself liable to demonic control. A demon could control even a child of God who abandoned conscious control of his own faculties and submitted himself to the movements of a board. In an innocuous way such as that Satan could gain access to the mind to control the thinking or to direct the course of action of an individual.

God and Satan are in a battle for the minds of men. It is the mind that Satan wants, for if he can control the mind he eventually can control the will. A battle goes on in the area of the mind as Satan seeks to subject us to these influences whereby we set aside the authority of the Word of God and seek something or someone else as a guide in our conduct. That is why the Apostle Paul can speak in I Timothy 4:1 and say, "The Spirit speaketh expressly, that in the latter times some shall depart from the faith, giving heed to seducing spirits, and doctrines of devils; speaking lies in hypocrisy." What Paul is saying is that just as soon as a man rejects the infallibility, the authority and the integrity of the Word of God and submits himself to the authority of men, he is rendering himself liable to satanic deception and satanic control in his thinking. The great tragedy today is that men feel qualified to sit in judgment upon the Word of God, accept what pleases them and reject what displeases them, little knowing that in this battle for minds Satan has gained a victory and has rendered them subject to demonic control. This battle is being waged today in the pulpit, where ministers of Satan have submitted themselves to satanic influence and they mouth the doctrines that are propagated by demons and are rejecting the Word of God. That is why the Apostle Paul places so much emphasis upon the mind. He says in Philippians 2:5: "Let this mind be in you" or "have the mind of Christ." He says in Philippians 4:8: "Whatsoever things are true, . . . honest . . . just . . . pure . . . lovely . . . of good report, *Think on these things.*" For as soon as a man forsakes the mind of Christ he is liable to demonic deception.

Many years ago when I was in seminary a national convention of spirit mediums was being held in the city of Dallas. At this convention mediums were contacting their controls, demons with whom they had contact, to bring messages to individuals. Six of us decided we would attend the meeting, which was announced as being open to the public. We walked into the darkened auditorium and quietly sat down in the rear to observe. The convention was called to order and the chairman of the meeting introduced different mediums who summoned their controls, the demons with whom they were on familiar terms. One after another attempted to make contact and failed, and sat down. Each announced that something was interfering with his making contact. There came a stir over the whole audience, for evidently they were not used to anything like this. The chairman got up, asked that the lights be turned on, and said there was some influence there that was preventing them from having contact with their familiar spirits. He pointed to us and said that that row of fellows back there was preventing them from establishing contacts. Before they could go on, we were asked to leave. We left. I would have liked to have known what happened after we left. But since the convention kept on for the rest of the week, I presume that, after we had gone, they were able to reestablish contact with the demons and to deceive and delude men's minds by demonic deception. The presence of the Spirit of God in the six believers prevented a manifestation of Satanic power.

It may seem strange to talk about something we can't see, feel, touch taste, smell. But you will not understand the nature of the warfare in which you as a child of God are engaged unless you recognize that Satan is warring to control your mind every moment of every day to deceive you concerning the truth of God. The very moment that you relax your hold on the authority of Scripture you are subject to satanic deception.

Do you remember what the Father said to the disciples on the Mount of Transfiguration? They had seen a great miracle there; they had seen Christ transformed before them. But Satan could empower men by demonic power to work miracles. God said to those disciples, "This is my beloved Son, hear ye him." There is no defense against satanic delusion and deception other than submission to the Word of Christ and the authority of the Person of Christ.

20

Satan's Destiny

Revelation 20:1 - 10

In June, 1967, war broke out between the Israelis and the Arabs. Because of its biblical significance, we followed the news attentively as it unfolded from day to day. It seemed from the reports emanating from Cairo that the Israelis were taking a terrific beating, for report after report came telling how many Israeli planes had been destroyed, how many tanks had been lost, how far the Egyptians had penetrated into Israel. The reports predicted that Egypt would be in Tel Aviv by night. For some days the war went on, Egypt still affirming its victories, announcing its triumphs. What was not known until hostilities ceased at the end of the week was that Israel, by destroying the air force and the air fields of the surrounding Arab states, had won complete victory within the first two hours of fighting. But the Arabs kept on fighting even though they were assured that they had been defeated.

The knowledge that one has been vanquished does not keep him from fighting. The fact that Satan has been defeated, his judgment pronounced, and his destiny settled does not keep him from waging warfare against God, against the Son of God, and against the children of God. The course of his warfare has been detailed for us in the Scriptures.

The Word of God has much to say concerning the destiny of Satan. We will study those portions of Scripture that reveal the execution of a judgment that has already been predetermined by God and by Jesus Christ. Back in John 12, our Lord announced to the disciples the certainty of His victory, and in a prophetic

183

revelation, He revealed that Satan was a vanquished foe. After our Lord had spoken of His death on the cross, likening that death to a kernel of wheat falling into the ground to die so that it might bring forth a great harvest, our Lord said: "Now is the judgment of this world: now shall the prince of this world be cast out. And I, if I be lifted up from the earth, will draw all men unto me." Our Lord who had just spoken of His death next speaks of His resurrection. When He said, "I, if I be lifted up from the earth" was not speaking of the cross where He was lifted up to die. He was speaking of the resurrection in which, by the Spirit of God, Jesus Christ would be lifted up from the grave, from the power of death and the power of Satan, and exalted at the right hand of God. And He promised that when He was lifted up He would draw all unto Him. Even from among those who had been drawn to Satan, our Lord says there will be those drawn to Him, for He is the victor over Satan. The resurrection is the proof of His victory. In the 31st verse, our Lord announced that judgment was to be passed upon Satan at the cross: "Now is the judgment of this world, now shall the prince of this world be cast out." The cross was God's judgment upon sin.

The death of Christ was the means and the cross of Christ was the place of judgment upon Satan. The adversary, who had begun his rebellion against God before the creation of this world, is now brought before the bar of judgment. By His death and resurrection Jesus Christ passed sentence upon the adversary of God. God who had to deal with the problem of sin by sending His Son to death must also deal with the problem of the author of sin. God who removed judgment from us by placing it upon another removed the adversary of our soul forever by removing him from the presence of God forever. The writers in the New Testament frequently refer to the judgment that was passed upon Satan and upon Satan's hosts at the cross.

In the epistle of Jude we find in verse 6: "The angels which kept not their first estate [those would be those created beings who had been servants of God but who rebelled against God along with Satan and joined Satan in his rebellion] but left their own habitation, he hath reserved in everlasting chains under darkness unto the judgment of the great day." A sentence has been passed, and those who followed Satan in his rebellion are under a judgment. Condemnation has been passed and God is awaiting the day of the execution of the judgment that has been set.

Peter speaks of this same judgment in II Peter 2:4: "If God spared not the angels that sinned [that would be a reference to the same fallen angels] but cast them down to hell, and delivered them into chains of darkness to be reserved under judgment. . . ." The fact that God passed judgment on angels is used by Peter to support the fact that God will judge men who are in rebellion against God. Peter views a judgment as having already been predetermined, but the time of the execution of that judgment is yet future.

We find a testimony of this fact in the response of demons to our Lord. It is recorded in Matthew 8:28 that as Christ went across the Sea of Galilee "into the country of the Gergesenes, there met him two possessed with devils, coming out of the tombs, exceeding fierce, so that no man might pass by that way." Now notice in verse 29 the involuntary response of demons to the Lord Jesus Christ: "Behold they cried out, saying, what have we to do with thee, [to translate that more literally, what do we have in common] thou Son of God; art thou come hither to torment us before the time?" These demons recognized that they were under judgment. They also recognized that Jesus Christ is the judge and it will be by the Word of His mouth that a predetermined judgment is meted out upon them and the sentence passed will be executed. They also know something of the program of God and the time that this will take place, for when Jesus Christ comes to this earth to reign, the first demonstration of His sovereign authority over the earth will be to bind Satan and to remove him from this sphere. They know then that their judgment and the coming of Christ to reign coincide. Since Jesus Christ is rejected by Israel at His first advent, they are smart enough to deduce that the time of this judgment has not arrived even though the Judge is personally present. So they address Christ by confessing that He is judge, confessing that they are under divine judgment, and acknowledging that the time will come when He will execute the sentence previously pronounced upon them.

In the twentieth chapter of the book of the Revelation, we have a description of the initial phase of the execution of the predetermined judgment. We read in Revelation 19:11-16 of the second advent of Jesus Christ to the earth, where He comes as a Victor, pictured as riding on a white horse. He bears the name King of kings and Lord of lords. And after subjugating nations that are in rebellion against Him at His second advent (Revelation 19:15), we read in Revelation 20:1: "I saw an angel come down from heaven, having the key of the bottomless pit and a great chain in his hand. He laid hold on the dragon, that old serpent, which is the Devil and Satan, and bound him a thousand years, and cast him into the bottomless pit, and shut him up, and set a seal upon him that he should deceive the nations no more, till the thousand years should be fulfilled." This we take to be a literal event.

It has been the opposition of Satan that has prevented the reign of the Lord Jesus Christ over this earth and the institution of the literal kingdom of God upon the earth. When the prophets offered a Messiah to Israel, Satan stirred up false prophets who denied the message of the prophets from God and turned Israel aside. When Jesus Christ came to offer Himself to Israel as her Messiah, it was Satan who stirred up religious leaders in opposition to Him, who persuaded the people that He was demon-possessed and a blasphemous imposter. Thus, the nation followed Satan's opposition and rejected Jesus Christ.

It is not until Jesus Christ comes to this earth the second time and binds Satan and removes Satan that it is possible for Jesus Christ to institute a reign of righteousness on this earth. Men have a fallen sin nature. Satan can still deceive men, even the saints of God. Satan can pervert men from the path of obedience to God and distort their affection and turn them aside from the love of God, and can blind their minds to the truth of God. Satan is active in his work of deception to prevent the literal and physical reign of Jesus Christ over this earth in that age we know as the Millennial Age. So when Jesus Christ comes to fulfill the purpose and the program of God to set up David's throne and to reign as David's Son from sea to sea and from shore to shore, it is necessary to remove our adversary, the Devil, the deceiver, from this scene. And Christ does it quite literally by binding Satan and sealing him up in a bottomless pit so that he cannot come forth during the time of our Lord's earthly reign to deceive the nations. And this earth will experience a reign of righteousness.

The binding of Satan is a sign to all heaven and to earth that Jesus Christ actually is King of kings and Lord of lords. God has authenticated Jesus Christ as the One who is the Son of God by the resurrection from the dead. And the resurrection is evidence to us that Jesus Christ is Saviour and Lord. But God will give another demonstration of the authority of Christ at the second advent. That demonstration is the binding and removing of Satan. The vast majority of miracles recorded in the gospels are in the realm of demonism, miracles dealing with deliverance of people who were blind or deaf or dumb because they were possessed by Satan's demons. That was an evidence to the nation of Israel that the authority of Christ exceeded the authority of Satan, for Christ could go into Satan's realm and remove those who were in bondage and grant them deliverance. It was a picture of what Christ will do when He comes the second time to reign.

We conclude that not only will Satan be removed but also all the demons who were subservient to him so that for the first time, since the fall of Adam, the world will be without demonic influences. And the reason that the earth can blossom as a rose is that it will not be blighted by Satan's weeds. The reason that men can live in righteousness and justice and peace is that the inhabitants will not be blighted by Satan's lies. Jesus Christ shall reign as King of kings and Lord of lords from sea to sea and from shore to shore because He has bound Satan.

But this is only the first step toward the final destiny of Satan. We read in Revelation 20:3 after the thousand years Satan must be loosed for a little season. Then the activity of Satan in the brief period in which he is loosed is described in verses 7 to 9. The earth whose population had been decimated by the wars of the Tribulation will experience a great population explosion during the millennial age. But those who are born in the millennial age are born with a fallen sin nature inherited from their parents. The millennial age is not heaven. The sin nature was not eradicated from those who go into the millennium. People go into this earthly reign with a fallen sin nature and their children are born with the same fallen nature. And they need to be saved.

The Gospel will be proclaimed across the length and breadth of the earth and Christ will be presented as the Saviour. Men can look upon Him who once was pierced for the sins of the world, and multitudes will come to know Christ through the ministry of the evangelists of God, the nation of Israel, who publish the good tidings of salvation through Christ in that day.

There will be numbers of little rebels who grow up and become big rebels. But they have evidence that to rebel against the authority of the King is to invite an immediate judgment of physical death, for Christ will immediately cut off anyone who rebels against Him and judge him with physical death. So there are multitudes, who because of the absence of an external temper and because of the fear of the judgment of death, remain outwardly in submission to the King but whose hearts are in rebellion. There is no opportunity to rebel. So to separate the saved from the unsaved, those who subject themselves to Christ from those who are rebels, the door of the bottomless pit is opened and Satan is loosed. He goes forth to do what he was prevented from doing the thousand years of Christ's earthly reign. He goes forth to deceive the nations, and that which worked so well once is attempted again. Satan repeats his previous sin and goes forth to deceive the nations to offer himself as a king and to promise that, if they follow him, he will deliver them from the obligation of being in subjection to Jesus Christ. And those who were rebels against Christ, now for the first time are able to join in rebellion against Him. They flock to this one whom they delight to acknowledge as their lord and their master, and trust that he will

deliver them from judgment by dethroning the Judge who reigns,
even the Lord Jesus Christ.

After this flurry of activity, we read in verse 10 of Satan's doom.
"The devil that deceived them was cast into the lake of fire and
brimstone, where the beast and false prophet are, and shall be
tormented day and night for ever and ever." Satan, all of the
angels who originally followed him in his rebellion against God,
together with all of the unbelieving rebels who lived during the
millennial age, are summarily dismissed from the presence of God
and are sent into the lake of fire and brimstone where they shall
be tormented day and night forever.

Our Lord frequently taught about the destiny of Satan. He
pointed out that Satan was consigned to a lake of fire that burneth
with brimstone. Our Lord taught that this lake was a literal place
into which the lost would be sent. He spoke of the intensity of
the sufferings of those who were in it. He also emphasized the
fact of the eternal loss of those who are separated from God and
are under divine judgment. Our Lord, the One whom we so often
think of as the gentle Jesus, was the One who more than any other
spoke of eternal punishment, revealed the destiny of Satan, and
warned individuals against participation in that destiny.

Many individuals question the eternality of the lake of fire.
When we speak of fire, we think of combustion, and the destruction of combustible material. Therefore, it is inconceivable that
there could be enough combustible material in the universe to
support an eternal fire. So, some take comfort in calculating how
long it would take to burn all the material in the universe, and
conclude that, when all the material in the universe has been
consumed, the fires of hell will cool down and there will be release from eternal punishment.

There is a phenomenon about which astronomers know very
little and are baffled, the phenomenon of dwarf white stars. These
are heavenly bodies that have gone through some contraction so
that the material substance of that body has been so compressed
that the amount of matter the size of a man's thumb would weigh
several tons. The compression of this matter into so small a com-
pass has created intense heat. The compression causes expansion

and the more the expansion, the greater the heat; and the heat reverses the process and causes contraction. The matter in these dwarf white stars can never cool off because the compression causes expansion, and the expansion generates heat, which in turn causes contraction. Astronomers say these dwarf white stars are in a permanent state in which, because of the pressure, all gases have been turned to liquids and all of the matter has been reduced to a molten state which can never change. The astronomer tells us then of the existence of heavenly bodies that from all of their calculations are literal lakes of fire that can never cool off.

We do not know whether one of these will be the designated place for Satan and his angels to be confined for eternity, but the astronomer does bear testimony to the truth that came from the lips of our Lord that God has prepared a place for the devil and his angels where they will suffer not only physically because of their surroundings, but certainly more than that, suffer in mind and body at what might have been. It is inconceivable that an angel in the lake of fire will not remember the privilege that was his before he first gave ear to the enticement of Lucifer and followed him in his rebellion. And in the midst of his torment, he certainly will cry out, "Oh, what it would have been if I had not listened to that one enticement, committed that one sin and followed Lucifer in his rebellion against God. I might today be serving in the presence of the God of the universe." Even those in hell will confess that Jesus Christ is Lord, is sovereign, has the right to be obeyed, and they will renounce all claims to sovereignty that Satan has made. But, alas, it is too late.

Our Lord warned that there are those who may join Satan in that place prepared for him and his angels. This earth was created to be a habitation for man. The lake of fire was created to be a habitation for Satan and his angels who had already rebelled against God before man was created. When Adam rebelled, his destiny was changed; he no longer had a right to the presence of God but joined with Satan and shared Satan's destiny, the lake of fire prepared for the devil and his angels. God in infinite grace provided a sacrifice for Adam, and God through Jesus Christ has provided a sacrifice for all of Adam's sons who, because of Adam's sin, are destined for the Lake of Fire to be separated from God for ever and ever. Through the death of Jesus Christ, He has provided for forgiveness of sins; He has provided a new home (the Father's home); He has provided a new destiny (the Father's presence); and He has provided the light of the Father's countenance to be our light rather than the light of the eternal Lake of Fire. The Lake of Fire was not prepared for any human being. It becomes their destiny because men join Satan in his rebellion. The Lake of Fire need not be your destiny, for Jesus Christ came to bring you to God by offering Himself as a sacrifice for the sin of the world. No salvation was provided for angels, for those who sinned with Satan were destined for the Lake of Fire with no hope or promise of salvation whatsoever. But God in grace has offered salvation to you. But the decision is yours: Heaven or the Lake of Fire? Jesus Christ or Satan?

The Apostle Paul, describing the glory that belongs to Jesus Christ, reminds us that when He became obedient unto death, even the death of the cross, "God also hath highly exalted him, and given him a name which is above every name: that at the name of Jesus every knee should bow, of things in heaven, and things in earth, and things under the earth; and that every tongue should confess that Jesus Christ is Lord, to the glory of God the Father" (Philippians 2:9 - 11). And in the unending ages of eternity no tongue will be lifted against the absolute authority of the Lord Jesus Christ. All heaven will confess Him as glorified Lord and Saviour. The unfallen angels will adore and serve Him. Even those banished from His presence will confess that the king whom they loved and served was an imposter and deceiver, and that Jesus Christ was the rightful Lord.

No one will rebel against His will, for all in heaven will recognize His authority and bow in obedience to Him. No other lord will invite submission, for Jesus Christ will rule as Lord forever. To Him be glory and honor, dominion and majesty, love and praise forever.

Design for Discipleship
Discovering God's Blueprint for the Christian Life

Discipleship may be a popular term in Christian circles, but what does it really mean? Pentecost demonstrates that discipleship is a growing experience of knowledge, commitment, active love, and service.

3451-3   128 pp.

The Joy of Living
A Study of Philippians

The apostle Paul wrote to the church at Philippi in order to help "make their joy complete." Contains helpful study and review questions for personal Bible study or sermon preparation.

3453-x   248 pp.

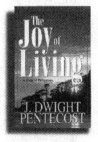

Things Which Become Sound Doctrine
Doctrinal Studies of Fourteen Crucial Words of Faith

Practical Christian living cannot be divorced from biblical knowledge. Fourteen key Bible doctrines including grace, repentance, sanctification, security, and predestination are explained in everyday terms.

3452-1   160 pp.

Thy Kingdom Come
*Tracing God's Kingdom Program and
Covenant Promises Throughout History*

Noted Bible teacher J. Dwight Pentecost traces the sweeping history of the kingdom program from eternity past to eternity future, relating it to the development of the covenant promises.

3450-5   360 pp.

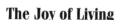

CPSIA information can be obtained
at www.ICGtesting.com
Printed in the USA
BVHW080123170719
553637BV00001B/83/P